How To Handle Tough Customers

Five 20-Minute Self-Study Sessions That Build the Skills You Need to Succeed

Featuring

Built-In Learning Reinforcement Tools

Case Studies

Personal Productivity Exercises

Customized Action Plans

Individualized Pre- and Post-Session Skill Assessments

COVER ILLUSTRATION: RANDALL ENOS

DARTNELL is a publisher serving the world of business with books, manuals, newsletters and bulletins, and training materials for executives, managers, supervisors, salespeople, financial officials, personnel executives, and office employees. Dartnell also produces management and sales training videos and audio cassettes, publishes many useful business forms, and many of its materials and films are available in languages other than English. Dartnell, established in 1917, serves the world's business community. For details, catalogs, and product information write:

THE DARTNELL CORPORATION
4660 N. Ravenswood Avenue
Chicago, IL 60640-4595, U.S.A.
Or phone (800) 621-5463 in U.S. and Canada

This publication is designed to provide accurate and authoritative information in regard to the subject matter covered. It is sold with the understanding that the publisher is not engaged in rendering legal, accounting, other professional service. If legal advice or other expert assistance is required, the services of a competent professional person should be sought.

—From a Declaration of Principles jointly adopted by a Committee of the American Bar Association and a Committee of Publishers.

ISBN #0-85013-287-8
Library of Congress #97-66739

Printed in the United States of America by the
Dartnell Press, Chicago, IL 60640-4595

INTRODUCTION

Dear Customer Service Professional:

You may find *How to Handle Tough Customers* somewhat different from comparable workbooks you have seen. That's because it *is* a little different, and intentionally so. Making a difference for you and your performance is what we hope to accomplish.

We were looking to create a highly interactive series of skill-developing exercises in a format that would be both entertaining and informative. We wanted to incorporate a system that could quantitatively define the skill improvements that might be achieved as a result of this workbook. And we wanted to bring the latest thinking, the most innovative techniques, and some unique insights to the attention of our own customers, the customer service professionals.

Tough Customers is in five chapters, or sessions, each of which should take approximately 20 minutes to complete. Each session features a series of short articles that are used as the basis for exercises. Each session contains tips and procedures for dealing with specific customer service problems. Each has a series of quizzes and tests designed to make the reader examine his or her own performance, attitude, and skill. And each session presents two Case Studies designed to make the readers think for themselves in dealing with the problem presented.

The Case Studies are intended to tap into the imaginations of the individuals examining them. You will notice that they become more difficult as the workbook progresses. In some instances there are no completely right or wrong answers; just as in the real working day of a customer service person, there are no hard and fast solutions to magically solving the problems that customers present.

The goals of the exercises and studies in this workbook are threefold: 1) to present customer service problems that most of the readers have encountered; 2) to present the skills and techniques that can be used to address the problems; and 3) to have the readers apply their own skills using the strategies presented to solve the problems.

As we said, this is an interactive workbook that will require a fair amount of involvement on your part. We hope you will bring your own ideas to solving the exercises. And we hope you have fun doing so.

In Session 1 of this workbook, we concentrate on *Understanding Tough Customers*. We look at what makes them tick, since understanding them is the first step to successfully dealing with them.

Session 2 concerns itself with *Calming Angry Customers and Solving Problems*. No one likes getting yelled at, but it sometimes comes with the territory. We explain what you can do.

In Session 3 we focus on a couple of specific situations: problems that arise with customers *Face to Face and On the Phone.* You'll see some situations that may look oddly familiar.

In Session 4 we deal with mistakes, both your own and those the customer won't own up to. The title for this fourth session is *Everybody Makes Mistakes (Can This Customer Be Saved?).*

And finally, in Session 5, we consider some ways to stop the trouble at the source. This one is titled *Preventing Customer Problems.*

So, there you have it. Now it's up to you to work your way through the instruction, cases, exercises, and self-assessments to take away the tips, techniques, and insights that will be most useful to you and your organization. We hope that both the content and self-paced, 20-minute module structure of *How to Handle Tough Customers* will help you achieve your goals in a way that is challenging, to be sure, but also enjoyable and clearly productive. The material included here was selected and adapted with care from materials developed by Dartnell's expert editorial staff and professional consultants in a variety of media, including books, newsletters, videos, and audiocassette tapes. Finally, if you have questions, comments, or suggestions about this workbook, or any others in *Dartnell's High-Performance Skill Builder Series* of workbooks, please call us at 800-621-5463 and ask for Customer Service.

CONTENTS

5 PREVENTING CUSTOMER PROBLEMS   73

1

UNDERSTANDING
TOUGH CUSTOMERS

INTRODUCTION

Working in customer service, you've no doubt found yourself on the receiving end of an irate customer's anger more times than you want to think about. It goes with the job.

Just the same, you're human too. Listening to the complaints, you find yourself getting angry in turn. And stressed out in the bargain.

What do these customers really want? Or don't want? What do they expect? What are they really saying? Or not saying? If only you could read their minds it would all be so much simpler.

You can't read their minds but you can learn to see things from their perspective. To deal effectively with tough customers you must first learn to understand them; not an easy job, for there are as many different kinds of customers as there are people. But if you can get a handle on them, you find the key to dealing with them — and to keeping yourself sane too.

Here's what you'll find in this first session of the *How to Handle Tough Customers*.

Skill Level Assessment I Think you're pretty good at what you do? Here's a test to find out.

Case Study: The Vanishing Customer Ever had a customer who one day just stopped doing business with you? For no reason at all? Here's why customers simply disappear and how to prevent that from happening to you.

Handling Complaints Effectively Four suggestions for solving an angry customer's problem, and a step-by-step method for implementing them using one of your own customers as a model.

The Customer's Top Four Wish List What are the four most important things every customer wants? Here they are.

Helping Uncertain Customers Sometimes customers have problems but don't even know what they want. What is it that will make them happy again?

How good are you at helping out uncertain customers? Here's how to find out.

Understanding Customers You Can't Understand Your customer isn't at a loss for words, but you're at a loss to understand. Is it because you're new to this business or industry and don't yet know the terminology? Or is the customer just in love with jawbreaking jargon? Either way, here are seven steps to quickly catch on, complete with a case study to practice them on.

Anger and Stress Can you keep your cool while your customers are losing theirs? Can you handle the stress they create within you? Here are a few suggestions for keeping your cool and handling stress, along with 10 ways for handling your own anger.

Personal Conflicts Mean Service Suicide An argument with your client? It's hard to think of a better way of damaging your career and yet it happens all the time. Do you know how to avoid customer conflicts? Find out.

Do You Remember? A short pop quiz to see how well you retained the information presented.

Skill Level Assessment II Are you learning to understand tough customers? To deal with them more effectively? To keep your own stress and anger under control? Take another look.

Action Plan Here's how to identify your strong points and weak ones — and a plan for turning those weaknesses into strengths.

With any good plan, you have to know where you are before you can figure out where you're going. Or how to get there. And that's precisely where this workbook session begins.

SKILL LEVEL ASSESSMENT I

Using the chart below, rate your own skills as they relate to the following statements.

WEAK	**AVERAGE**	**STRONG**
1–4 Points	5–7 Points	8–10 Points

Recognize that there are different types of customers.   _____

Understand your own customers.   _____

Know what customers are looking for.   _____

Ask questions when faced with a complaint.   _____

Show interest when a customer complains.   _____

Focus on the problem.   _____

Know how to prevent customer complaints.   _____

Remain cool when confronted by angry customers.   _____

Understand why a customer is angry.   _____

Show ability to empathize with angry customers.   _____

Control your own anger when faced with tough customers.   _____

Know how to manage stress caused by complaining customers.   _____

Show ability to avoid conflicts with customers.   _____

TOTAL RATING: _____

WEAK	**FAIR**	**GOOD**	**STRONG**
Under 52	53–77	78–103	104–130

Unless you're "super-rep" — or less than forthright in your self-evaluation — the chances are good that improvement is possible. Let's see what we can do about that.

John was in a state of shock. His boss just called him in and told him that Bill, one of John's most reliable customers, had phoned that morning to say that he would now be doing business with one of their competitors. Bill had not given any particular reason for taking his business elsewhere other than to say he had been unhappy with John's company for some time now. He had not even seemed angry or upset.

John cannot believe it. He had never had a complaint from Bill, or even suspected something was wrong. Bill was always all business and never so much as hinted that he was displeased with the way John handled his account. And now John learns that he's had a gripe all this time. Why didn't he ever say anything?

There are three kinds of customers:
1) those who constantly nag and complain;
2) those who complain infrequently;
3) those who never complain.

Type 3 customers, those who never complain, *are the ones who should concern you the most.* Almost every customer has a problem or a complaint from time to time. Type 3 customers, though, never seem to complain and usually seem content with your service. These customers don't like conflict, don't like making waves even when they're annoyed. Those annoyances may fester and grow — turning to outright anger — and you still may have no idea they're displeased with you.

When these types of customers get fed up they don't protest and argue, they simply take their business elsewhere — and never come back.

List three things you could do, or could have done, to prevent these "silent" customers from growing angry enough to take their business away from you. Here's a clue: The key word is prevention.

1. _____

2. _____

3. _____

(Answers appear at the end of this chapter on page 13.)

ANSWER THE FOLLOWING QUESTIONS WITH A   YES OR NO.

1. Do you have a customer who has never complained to you? About anything? Ever? ❏   ❏

2. Do you have a customer who is easy-going, or the quiet type? The kind of person who hates conflict? ❏   ❏

3. Think of a customer with whom everything is going well. Are you *certain* he or she is well-pleased with you and your company? ❏   ❏

If you answered **YES** to any of the questions, you might want to take a little action. Check the answer section for a few tips on how to proceed.

HANDLING COMPLAINTS EFFECTIVELY

In some ways it's easier to deal with a customer who does complain. At least you know where you stand, even if it's temporarily on shaky grounds. Here's an exercise for handling those complaints effectively to put you and your company back on solid footing.

Think of a recent complaint an angry customer brought to you. Briefly describe the customer's problem:

_____

_____

_____

Here are some suggestions for dealing with angry customers. After each one, write down what you did (or didn't do) with your angry customer as it relates to the suggestion.

1. **Try to identify the type of customer (person) you are dealing with to learn how to successfully communicate with him or her.**

_____

_____

_____

2. Ask questions to get the information you need to solve the problem quickly.

_____

_____

_____

3. Know what your customer expects from you when he or she complains. If you're uncertain, ask.

_____

_____

_____

4. Know when to refer a customer to another source to solve the problem.

_____

_____

_____

Were you able to successfully solve the customer's problem? How?

_____

_____

_____

Was the customer still angry afterward? Do you think the customer will continue doing business with you or your company? Why?

_____

_____

_____

Based on what you've learned from these suggestions, what would you do differently the next time a similar situation occurs?

_____

_____

_____

THE CUSTOMER'S TOP FOUR WISH LIST

Here are a customer's top four needs:

1. **Value for their money.**
2. **Solutions to their problems.**
3. **Concern for their needs.**
4. **Answers to their questions.**

It's a good list to memorize — not to mention that it will probably show up again later in this session.

QUIZ

HELPING UNCERTAIN CUSTOMERS

It's easy to follow routine instructions. But when a customer is uncertain, it's a challenge to customer service reps to use their imagination and initiative. Take the following quiz to test your take-charge abilities.

	YES	NO
1. When problems occur, are you usually confident in your ability to think for yourself?	❏	❏
2. As a rule, do you ask questions about things you don't understand or that don't make sense to you?	❏	❏
3. Do you feel it's part of your job to give guidance to customers as well as routine service?	❏	❏
4. Do you ask for specifics regarding a customer's problem?	❏	❏
5. Are you self-assured and self-reliant in your role as a customer service rep?	❏	❏
6. Do you let uncertain customers know what their options are by making suggestions?	❏	❏
7. Do you arm yourself with information about your company and its products?	❏	❏
8. Do you look for ways to provide service that even demanding customers don't expect?	❏	❏
9. If you don't know what a customer's options are, do you ask someone who does?	❏	❏
10. Do you convey that you have the customer's best interests at heart, then set out to prove it?	❏	❏

Total Number of YES Answers _____

A total of eight or more **YES** answers indicates that you can take charge of an uncertain customer and guide him or her to a solution. A lower score indicates that you might flounder if a customer isn't specific with his or her demands. Ask your boss about steps you can take to help uncertain customers.

UNDERSTANDING CUSTOMERS YOU CAN'T UNDERSTAND

CUSTOMER: *"We have decided to give a marginally higher utility and durability rating to the product evaluated as consistent with our enhanced analytical standards."*

YOU: *"Oh (long pause) … good."*

Sometimes a customer isn't shy about expressing needs but, owing to poor communication skills or a fascination with jargon, he or she may as well be speaking a foreign language.

Clear communication is a prerequisite to building effective customer relationships. To open those lines of communication, you are going to have to learn to speak their language. To do that you must learn to translate what they're saying and show that you understand it. Here's how:

1. Demonstrate your interest. Listen intently, and let your responses show you're involved in the conversation — even if you're struggling to understand its implications.

2. Listen for key words. As your customer is speaking, what words and phrases recur? Where is the verbal emphasis placed? By listening for the key words and the context of those words, the meaning may become clearer.

3. Ask for examples. Never fake understanding. Instead, ask the customer to give you an example, to describe a specific case. Even the most abstract or convoluted idea becomes clearer when it's stated in terms of an example.

4. Ask for advice. Never say, "I just don't understand what you're talking about." Rather, ask your customer for help: "How do you think I can apply this principle as I work with you?" Or, "What do you think I can do to get a better handle on what you're describing?"

5. Do some research. Read as much as you can about your customers' industries and businesses. This will help you learn the jargon of the business as well as the day-to-day problems they might face.

6. Relate your customer's comments to your own experience. For example, you might compare your customer's quality-assurance program procedures to your customer-service ones. This technique helps to establish common ground.

7. Exercise your growing expertise. As you learn to understand your customers, offer suggestions using their own terminology.

CASE #2: THE CLIENT FROM MARS

Helen excitedly made her way into the conference room for the meeting. Her company had just won a new account and she was the customer service person assigned to work on the account. Today she was meeting with the new client's marketing people to get started. Helen had never worked on an account in this particular industry before, but she wasn't worried. She had always been a fast study and knew things would work out fine.

An hour later she wasn't so sure. The marketing director's presentation was laced with industry jargon that Helen couldn't make heads or tails of. How was she supposed to carry on an intelligent conversation if she didn't know what they were talking about?

Use the seven points just discussed to work through the following case.

Write down a business or industry you have never worked in (but may one day) or one that you were unfamiliar with when you first started.

_____

_____

_____

Assume the customer has just explained something you don't truly understand — and continues to talk on. Write down a phrase or two you could say to **demonstrate your interest**.

_____

_____

_____

List a few **key words or phrases** that you might expect to (or did) hear that were completely new to you.

_____

_____

_____

Using the key word or phrase, frame a question to **ask for an example** the customer could give you to clarify the phrase.

_____

_____

_____

In your own speaking style, write down a phrase that would **ask the customer for advice** on how to better understand what he or she is describing.

_____

_____

_____

List several sources that would enable you to **do some research** on the business or industry you selected.

_____

_____

_____

Taking one of the customer's key words or comments, try to **relate it to something in your own experience**.

_____

_____

_____

Using your **growing expertise,** frame a suggestion to the customer using the key words or phrases you listed above.

_____

_____

_____

Keeping Your Cool When Customers Let Anger Flare Angry customers can create stress and anger for you. Even the best customer service professional can sometimes find that stress to be overwhelming. It is then that you may let your anger show.

Anger is your worst enemy. How can you control it? Here are three simple techniques to practice when talking to an angry customer.

- Take slow, deep breaths to calm yourself.

- Focus on the facts.

- Empathize with the customer.

What techniques do you use? What others can you think of that you might use? Make a list of techniques you can employ to deal with your own anger.

1. _____

2. _____

3._____

4. _____

5. _____

6. _____

7._____

8. _____

9._____

10. _____

How many did you think of? Which ones do you think would work for you? For a full list turn to the **ANSWERS SECTION** on page 13.

PERSONAL CONFLICTS MEAN SERVICE SUICIDE

The fastest way to lose customers (and any referrals from them) is to argue. Do you avoid customer conflict? Take the following quiz to find out.

	YES	NO
1. Do you feel your customers' opinions are less important than your own?	❏	❏
2. Can you exit a disagreement gracefully?	❏	❏
3. Do you carefully phrase statements and opinions you relate to customers?	❏	❏
4. Can you accept that customers' opinions might not always match your own?	❏	❏
5. Can you separate the customer from his or her statement?	❏	❏
6. Do you understand the difference between being assertive and being aggressive?	❏	❏
7. Do you base your statements on fact, not conjecture?	❏	❏
8. Do you feel that you are always right and that it's the customer's responsibility to prove you're wrong?	❏	❏
9. Do you agree with everything customers say, no matter how outlandish their statements may be?	❏	❏
10. Can you and do you readily admit when you've made a mistake?	❏	❏

Total Number of YES Answers _____

Give yourself a point for each correct answer. All questions require a **YES** answer except numbers 1, 8, and 9.

SCORE: _____

9–10 points: Expert avoider. You are tactful when it comes to customer conflict. You understand how detrimental customer conflict can be to your company's sales — and your career.

7–8 points: Diplomat. You usually avoid conflict. But be careful not to get baited into an argument. Put yourself in the customer's place.

0–6 points: Clasher. You have a tendency to get into conflict. You may be spending too much time arguing or proving you're right. It's time to rethink what your actual service role is.

CASE #1: THE VANISHING CUSTOMER

Here are the three ways you can prevent "silent" customers from becoming angry enough to take their business away from you.

The key is prevention. Check in with your uncommunicative customers from time to time and probe these three areas:

1. **General attitude. (Ask, "Is everything going okay?")**

2. **Look for trouble spots. ("Do you have any problems with our service?")**

3. **Offer assistance. ("Can you use any help?")**

10 WAYS TO DEAL WITH YOUR OWN ANGER

1. **Write down your feelings.**

2. **Draw cartoons of how the customer looks to you. (Refrain from laughing or grinning.)**

3. **Predetermine not to get angry.**

4. **Focus on long-range goals.**

5. **"Kill" them with kindness.**

6. **Depersonalize the situation by classifying the customer's behavioral style.**

7. **Remember the anger is not directed at you personally. (The customer is angry at the situation.)**

8. **Always speak in a positive manner.**

9. **Refrain from using an accusatory tone.**

10. **Be careful in your choice of words.**

D O   Y O U   R E M E M B E R ?

Can you recall the four top customer needs mentioned earlier in this session? (Refer to page 7.)

1. _____

2. _____

3. _____

4. _____

Can you recall the three different types of customers as they relate to complaints? (Refer to page 4.)

1. _____

2. _____

3. _____

Which one of those three should you concern yourself with the most?

_____

Can you name any four of the seven ways to facilitate clear communication when you are having difficulty understanding what your customer is saying? (Refer to page 8.)

1. _____

2. _____

3. _____

4. _____

Based upon what you have learned in Session 1, rate yourself on the following statements. When you are finished, compare your rating to the one you earned at the beginning of this session.

WEAK   **AVERAGE**   **STRONG**

1–4 Points   5–7 Points   8–10 Points

Recognize that there are different types of customers. _____

Understand your own customers. _____

Know what customers are looking for. _____

Ask questions when faced with a complaint. _____

Show interest when a customer complains. _____

Focus on the problem. _____

Know how to prevent customer complaints. _____

Remain cool when confronted by angry customers. _____

Understand why a customer is angry. _____

Show ability to empathize with angry customers. _____

Control your own anger when faced with tough customers. _____

Know how to manage stress caused by complaining customers. _____

Show ability to avoid conflicts with customers. _____

TOTAL RATING: _____

WEAK   **FAIR**   **GOOD**   **STRONG**

Under 52   53–77   78–103   104–130

A C T I O N   P L A N

Many of the skills discussed are interrelated, and building from your strengths is a good place to start improving your overall abilities. But you can't afford to overlook your weaknesses either. List below your three best scores (your **strengths**) and your three lowest scores (your **weaknesses**) from the ratings on the previous page.

STRENGTHS

1. _____

2. _____

3. _____

WEAKNESSES

1. _____

2. _____

3. _____

Comparing the two lists, can you see any ways in which you can use your strengths to improve your weaknesses? If so, write them down briefly.

_____

_____

_____

_____

_____

Now re-examine your three biggest weaknesses. Since it's best to work on them one at a time, list them in this order: Start with the one you think will be the easiest to improve upon, followed by a more difficult one, and then the most difficult one. Next to each, set a timetable for concentrating on them (one week, two weeks, etc.).

T I M E T A B L E   F O R   W O R K I N G   O N
W E A K N E S S E S / I M P R O V E M E N T

1. _____

2. _____

3. _____

Using the ideas and information from this session, list at least one technique you can practice to improve each weakness. Also add any ideas of your own.

1. _____

2. _____

3. _____

If you cannot determine a technique or course of action you think will be effective, talk to your supervisor for ideas that can be applied to your specific situation.

At the end of the time frame you set for improvement on *all* of your weaknesses, look again at the skill level rating on page 15. Rate yourself once more on *all* of the statements listed. You will probably find improvement not only in your weak areas but in *all* of the others as well.

S U M M A R Y

Tough customers make a customer service representative's job all that much more difficult. It takes a combination of insight and understanding — along with a great deal of patience — to successfully handle their complaints. It also takes a special kind of person with a special set of skills to defuse a customer's anger and to solve his or her problem at the same time.

This first session has concentrated on the skills needed to recognize what customers want and expect, and how to prevent their anger from becoming your anger. It has emphasized that customers and their complaints come in all shapes and sizes, that not all tough customers are complainers, that customers have their own sets of expectations and ways of doing business, and that they can be uncertain or demanding or anywhere in between.

It's up to you to adapt.

Sometimes just solving the immediate problem will be enough. Other times the customer himself is the problem. Knowing what those chronically difficult customers want and expect is the only way to fulfill them — and the only way to turn tough customers into satisfied ones. The skills practiced in Session 1 will help.

In the next session we'll begin to focus on more specific situations, including how to calm angry customers and how to present problem-solving solutions.

CALMING ANGRY CUSTOMERS AND SOLVING PROBLEMS

INTRODUCTION

Dealing with angry customers sometimes requires the skills of a diplomat, the patience of a saint, and the problem-solving ability of a detective. In short, it requires a true customer service professional.

Session 2 provides the opportunity to enhance some of the skills you already possess and presents some new techniques and strategies for calming angry customers and for coming up with solutions to their problems. It also explains why these approaches work and offers tips on when and how to apply them.

Obviously, it's not easy to remember what you should do when someone is screaming at you. That's why the approach you take has to be all but instinctive. And to be instinctive, it has to be a learned skill you can draw upon when needed. The case studies and exercises in this session will allow you to practice these techniques and, in time, develop them into a basic part of your customer service repertoire.

Here's what we'll be covering in Session 2:

Skill Level Assessment I How good are you at calming angry customers? At finding solutions to their problems? At sending them away satisfied? Check yourself out.

Cooling Down a Customer Here's a strategic approach for cooling down angry customers, complete with a case study to help you perfect the technique.

Different Strokes for Different Customers Not all tough customers are angry but that doesn't make them any easier to handle. Here's how to recognize and interact with them successfully.

Quick Tips A few words of wisdom to remember when those furious customers come calling.

Can You Take It? When the tough customers keep coming, that constant barrage of criticisms and complaints can weary anyone. How tough are you? Here's how to find out.

Developing a Knack for Handling Complaints Is it a natural talent? A perfected skill? Or a little bit of both? Here's a method you can use to develop that customer-pleasing knack for solving problems. A case study is provided to help you get the *knack* for it.

Turnabout Is Fair Play Here's the biggest challenge of all: turning that angry, complaining customer into a happy, complacent one. Are you up to it? It may not be as difficult as you think.

Five Rules for Better Customer Service Five quick tips every customer service professional should know.

Win-Win Solutions Work for Customers Are you on the lookout for solutions that will benefit both your client and your company? Do you know how to go about it? Here's how to tell.

Do You Remember? Our session-ending pop quiz.

Skill Level Assessment II Are you improving your ability to calm angry customers? To find solutions to their problems? To send them away satisified? Take another look.

Action Plan Here's how to identify your strong points and weak ones — and a plan for turning those weaknesses into strengths.

Calming a customer down won't necessarily solve his or her problem. Solving the problem doesn't necessarily cool down a customer. The two issues are inseparably linked, and the only way to completely satisfy an angry customer is to perform both tasks.

Now let's go about finding ways to do it.

SKILL LEVEL ASSESSMENT I

Using the chart below, rate your own skills as they relate to the following statements:

WEAK	**AVERAGE**	**STRONG**
1–4 points	5–7 points	8–10 points

Show ability to cool down angry customers. _____

Find out what a complaining customer wants. _____

Ask for details of a complaint; get the story straight. _____

Apologize to a customer even when it's not your own fault. _____

Deal well with obstinate customers. _____

Know what to do when customers become angry. _____

Handle complaints and criticisms directed at you. _____

Have a knack for dealing with complaints. _____

Show ability to turn dissatisfied customers into satisfied ones. _____

Attend to customers' problems quickly. _____

Work to develop win-win solutions for customers and clients. _____

Follow up with customers after resolving complaints. _____

TOTAL RATING _____

WEAK	**FAIR**	**GOOD**	**STRONG**
Under 48	49–65	66–84	85–120

A score under 65 means there's room for improvement. A score between 66–84 shows you're doing well but can do better. Any score over 85 means it's just a matter of building on your strengths.

A customer calls in the heat of rage — yelling and screaming at you — and you're caught off guard. The person seems irrational and there appears to be no way to calm him or her down. What do you do?

When a customer is hot under the collar, you need all the composure you can muster. Why? Because it's not always simple to keep the facts straight.

To cool the customer's anger and solve the problem to everyone's satisfaction, try the following procedure:

1. Grab a pad. It's critical that you get the facts straight. Keep detailed notes of the conversation. And tell the customer you're doing so. This gives him or her a feeling of empowerment.

2. Ask for details. To get a grip on the problem, get feedback from the caller. Focus on a description of events rather than the customer's interpretation of them.

3. Relate the incident back. Retell the facts as you understand them. Ask the caller to verify them or fill in any missing information.

4. Ask for a remedy. In short, what does the customer expect you to do about the problem? The customer's expectations should take top priority. Realize that you might have to negotiate the terms if he or she asks for the moon.

5. Don't internalize the anger. Always remember that the caller is probably angry about the situation, not with you personally. (Sometimes, that's not an easy distinction to make.)

C A S E   # 1 :   T H E   M I S S I N G   O R D E R

An order a customer placed with Jane's company has not yet been delivered. Jane did not take the customer's order and knew nothing about it until now.

The enraged customer phones. This is what Jane hears:

"You people promised me I'd have it Tuesday — Wednesday at the very latest and here it is Wednesday night and tomorrow's Thursday and I still don't have the (expletive deleted) thing and I'm leaving town for a major presentation this weekend and I absolutely must have it in time to take with me. I told you people when I ordered it last Thursday that if you couldn't get it to me by Wednesday I'd go someplace else but you insisted it would be here Tuesday and if I knew you couldn't get it to me like you promised I would have gone somewhere else in the first place!"

Using the five points just discussed, write down what you would say and do to calm the customer and solve the problem.

1. **Grab a pad. What do you say?**

2. **Ask for details.**

3. **Relate the incident back.**

4. **Ask for a remedy.**

5. **Don't internalize the anger. (What do you say to *yourself*?)**

Suggested remarks are listed in the **ANSWERS SECTION** on page 32.

DIFFERENT STROKES
FOR DIFFERENT CUSTOMERS

Anyone who serves customers, whether in-house or in the field, must play a variety of roles. Depending on the situation, there are times when you must be sympathetic or apologetic, and times when you must stand firm or give ground. In all of these situations, you must exercise sensitivity and tact.

- **The exploding customer.** When a customer is in the heat of anger, your smartest move is to keep your mind open and your mouth shut. The longer you allow the customer to let off steam, the faster the anger will diffuse. Listen sympathetically for as long as seems reasonable. When you reply, do so calmly and as helpfully as possible. If you cannot solve the problem immediately, assure the customer that you will give the matter your swift and most caring attention. Then, report back to the customer as soon as possible.

- **The obstinate customer.** Faced with unreasonable demands? Your first impulse is probably to argue. Remember that winning the argument but losing the customer makes for bad business. Even if you convince the customer that a request or demand is unreasonable, your company loses potential revenue. What do you do? Go along with the customer up to a point. Agree that his or her position has merit. Then calmly present fact-based, persuasive reasons why you cannot comply. (Do **not** use the phrase *"It's against company policy."* Customers tend to view that as an excuse rather than a reason — and they're often right.) Then explain what you *can* do to help. Often this will satisfy the customer's demands. If you're not qualified or authorized to deal with the problem, contact your manager.

- **The credit risk.** Let's say the customer wants to place an order but the amount exceeds his or her authorized credit limit. Or perhaps the customer is on the "reject" list. Few things are more embarrassing than being turned down for credit. So don't treat this person like a leper. Who knows? Today's poor risk might be tomorrow's good customer. Be friendly and respectful. If the customer challenges your turndown, explain politely that you'll check into the matter — or let the credit department do the explaining.

- **The customer who goofs up.** Never take an "I told you so" attitude with a customer, even if it's the customer who made the mistake. Why add to his or her embarrassment? Your best bet is to assure the customer that it's a mistake anybody could have made. (That customer doesn't have to know it's the weirdest mistake you have ever seen.) Minimize the mistake's importance to maximize your customer's effectiveness.

What Would You Do?

Based on what you have just read in "Different Strokes for Different Customers," list at least one thing you would do, and one thing you would not do, with each of the following different types of customers. (List more than one if you can.)

THE EXPLODING CUSTOMER

Would do

_____

_____

_____

Would not do

_____

_____

_____

THE OBSTINATE CUSTOMER

Would do

_____

_____

_____

Would not do

_____

_____

_____

THE CREDIT RISK

Would do

_____

_____

_____

Would not do

_____

_____

_____

THE CUSTOMER WHO GOOFS UP

Would do

_____

_____

_____

Would not do

_____

_____

_____

FOUR HELPFUL HINTS
FOR CALMING ANGRY CUSTOMERS

1. Eye to eye. Maintain eye contact when trying to calm an angry customer. Be sure your expression, body position, and gestures show your concern.

2. Say No to Boredom. Customers may spend a lot of time sounding off about a complaint. And complaints can have a sameness to them. But never forget that the future of the company is in your customers' hands. Listen patiently. Let them know you consider their problem important.

3. Whisper. Is an angry customer speaking loudly to you? If you speak more softly, the caller is likely to follow suit. (Try it. You'll be surprised how effective this simple technique can be.)

4. Combat a complainer. When you know you can satisfy a disgruntled customer, offer your "make right" plan immediately. Say: "Please allow me to make this right by … " That helps keep angry feelings from building up momentum.

Try to keep these four tips in mind. (We'll be asking about them later in this session.)

CAN YOU TAKE IT?

Problems, complaints, criticism … it's coming at you from every direction. Can you handle all this adversity? Take this quiz and find out.

	YES	NO
1. Are you sensitive to the problems and pressures of others?	❏	❏
2. Do you view superior service as your number one responsibility?	❏	❏
3. Do you appreciate the reality that you are never too smart or too old to learn?	❏	❏
4. Do you consider complaints from the complainer's point of view?	❏	❏
5. Do you generally make it your business to learn from constructive criticism?	❏	❏
6. Do you agree that even if you win an argument with a customer you end up losing?	❏	❏
7. Do you make it a conscious habit to smile in the face of adversity?	❏	❏
8. Do you look upon the mistakes you make as learning experiences?	❏	❏
9. Do you always try to be reasonable when you feel provoked to lambast others?	❏	❏
10. Do you appreciate the reality of business life that the more important your job, the more flak you're likely to get day to day?	❏	❏

Total Number of YES Answers _____

How did you do? A score of 9 or 10 **YES** answers rates you as well-adjusted and tough; 7 or 8 is well above average; 6 is fair. Any score lower than 6 indicates the hardening process still has a long way to go. Grit your teeth and strengthen your resolve to remain thoughtful and cool.

DEVELOPING A KNACK FOR HANDLING COMPLAINTS

Have you ever had a co-worker who just seemed to have a knack for resolving complaints? Ever wondered why he or she seemed to do it so effortlessly? Chances are good that that co-worker actually had a finely tuned sense of what would and wouldn't work, and a skillful procedure for acting on that intuition.

You can develop that knack, too, by learning these seven easy steps for handling complaints.

1. Find out exactly what the complaint is. Don't assume anything. Hear the person out. Once you fully understand what went wrong and why — and if you feel the problem is correctable — *make suggestions on what might work.* For example, you might say, "Are you sure it is plugged in?" If you can't solve the problem on the spot, move on to step 2.

2. Find out what the customer wants you to do about it. Some customers who complain just want you to hear them out. "Well, I'm sure I'll figure out these instructions in the next few minutes, but I did want somebody with your company to understand how complicated they are," a customer may say.

On the other hand, some customers will demand more than your company can give. In such cases, say, "Although I'm not in a position to grant that request, I can offer you … "

3. Decide if the complaint is valid and, if you can, fulfill the customer's request. Unless you have good reason to think otherwise, consider the complaint valid. Only when you hear things that don't jibe should you suspect a con job; if the suggestion for rectifying the situation is reasonable, keep the customer happy and comply.

4. Tell the customer exactly what you can and cannot do in handling the complaint. And offer to refer the complaint to a higher party if what you can do for the person is unacceptable.

5. Get the customer's name, telephone number, address, order number, and any other particulars, if you haven't already done so.

6. In instances where you cannot satisfy the complainer by your words or actions, refer the complaints to the person or department that can. Then follow up to make certain that the customer has been served.

7. Try to keep the customer happy.

CASE #2: THE WARM REFRIGERATOR AND THE HOT CUSTOMER

Doug was used to annoyed customers but this one was livid. She had purchased a refrigerator and it was delivered this morning. "But that was four hours ago," she screams, "and the refrigerator still isn't cooling."

"I can't make heads or tails of the instruction book," she says in an ominous tone, "and somebody there had better fix this for me or there's going to be real trouble."

Using the seven steps just discussed, Doug manages to solve the problem. Write down what you think he said.

1. _____

2. _____

3. _____

4. _____

5. _____

6. _____

7. _____

Suggested remarks are listed in the **ANSWERS SECTION** on page 32.

TURNABOUT IS FAIR PLAY

The biggest test of your customer service skills is your ability to turn dissatisfied customers into satisfied ones. Often, this is not as difficult as it sounds. Sometimes customers realize that the problem is not your fault — they may even admit the problem is their own fault — and can become grateful if the problem is solved in a friendly and helpful manner.

Other times the problem does lie with you or your company's product or service, and these situations can get quite touchy. Here's how to turn around those difficult situations.

• **Attend to the problem quickly.** The longer customers wait for you to respond to a problem, the angrier and more impatient they become. If you attend to the customer's problem immediately, you can save the sale and the customer.

• **Always see the customer's side.** Hearing complaints is never easy. But resist the urge to become defensive. Don't get upset or shift blame to the customer. Do your best to provide a remedy.

• **Go beyond the call of duty.** No job manual can allow for every contingency. But if customers are unhappy about a product or service, it's your responsibility to make things right. Find out what it takes to solve the problem — and keep the customer coming back.

• **Follow up.** Even if a problem has been settled, it's smart to ensure that it has by making a brief call or sending a short note of apology and explanation. Let your customer know you're genuinely sorry for any inconvenience. Show that you work for a company that truly cares about its clients.

Think of a situation in which you successfully resolved a complaint and turned an annoyed or angry customer into a satisfied one. Briefly state the customer's problem below.

_____

_____

_____

Now write down the various steps you took in handling the problem.

_____

_____

_____

_____

Think for a moment about the actions you took as they relate to the four guidelines mentioned previously. Which of them did you apply to your resolution of the problem?

_____

_____

_____

Which, if any, did you not?

_____

_____

_____

If you had it to do over again, would you do anything differently? If so, what?

_____

_____

_____

FIVE RULES FOR BETTER CUSTOMER SERVICE

1. Remember, the client isn't the enemy.

2. Avoid treating customers as if the problems are their fault.

3. Return all calls within 24 hours.

4. In person, acknowledge customers quickly.

5. Whether small or big spenders, all customers deserve to be treated equally.

Keep these five rules in mind. (They are almost certain to come in handy later.)

QUIZ

WIN-WIN SOLUTIONS WORK FOR CUSTOMERS

Customer service can become a struggle of wills. But Stephen R. Covey, in *The Seven Habits of Highly Effective People* (Simon and Schuster), tells about using the "win-win" strategy in interpersonal relations. Some of those ideas can be applied to your customer-service work. Try this test and score yourself honestly.

	YES	NO
1. When discussions get hot, do I try to see the problem from the customer's point of view?	❏	❏
2. Do I make a pointed effort to find out what my customer's needs are?	❏	❏
3. Do I make a list of my client's needs when discussing a problem?	❏	❏
4. Can I effectively separate my client's concerns from his or her demands on an issue?	❏	❏
5. Do I determine what will solve the problem?	❏	❏
6. Can I think of different solutions to offer?	❏	❏
7. Do I present those different solutions in a spirit of trying to mutually solve the problem?	❏	❏
8. Do I remember to use terms and language that promote a win-win approach?	❏	❏
9. Do I ignore heated statements and loaded charges made by my client?	❏	❏
10. Do I refrain from placing blame on anyone?	❏	❏

Total Number of YES Answers _____

Eight to 10 **YES** answers indicate you're really trying to work out mutually satisfactory agreements. The lower your score, the more you're into "brinksmanship" — and the more stress you have in dealing with clients. Read the questions again and apply the pointers discussed. You'll be satisfied and find yourself a "winner."

CASE #1: The Missing Order

1. Grab your pad and pen. Now let the customer know you're taking notes. "Okay, let me just write everything down here. I want to be sure I get the facts straight."

2. Ask for details. "Now this was to be shipped out to you, correct? And you were told you would have it today, Wednesday, at the latest. Is that right? Do you recall who you spoke with here about this?"

3. Relate the incident back. "Okay, so you placed the order last Thursday, it was promised to you by today, Wednesday. And you're leaving town Friday and need it to take with you."

4. Apologize. "First of all, let me say that I'm very sorry about this mix-up."

5. Ask for a remedy. "How can we fix this for you? Would you like us to deliver it to whatever hotel you'll be staying at if we can't get it to you before you leave town?"

6. Don't internalize the anger. Say to yourself: "He's not mad at me personally. I'm just the person who happened to take the call and he needs to blow off steam. Can't say I blame him. Actually, if I can fix this for him in time he'll probably be grateful to me."

DEVELOPING   A   KNACK
FOR   HANDLING   COMPLAINTS

CASE #2: The Warm Refrigerator and the Hot Customer

1. Find out exactly what the complaint is. "OK, so the refrigerator is running but it's not cooling — is that right?"

2. Find out exactly what the customer wants you to do about it. "How would you like me to fix this for you?" Or, "What's the best way to fix this for you?"

3. Decide if the complaint is valid and if you can fulfill the customer's request. "I can tell you have a real problem on your hands. There are a couple of things I can do for you."

4. Tell the customer exactly what you can and cannot do in handling the complaint. "Now I can't ship a second refrigerator out to you just like that. But I can get one of our service people back out to your home to look it over. Or, I can put you in touch right now with someone from our technical staff."

5. Get the customer's name, telephone number, address, order number, and any other particulars if you haven't already done so. "Let me just get your name, address, and phone number first. Do you have the order number handy?"

6. In instances where you can't satisfy the complainer by your words or actions, refer the complaints to the person or department that can. "It sounds like it just may be that something or other isn't adjusted or turned on or set up properly ."I'm going to transfer you to someone in our technical department."

7. Try to keep the customer happy. "I'm going to call you back to check and see if they solved this for you, okay?"

D O   Y O U   R E M E M B E R ?

Remember the four helpful hints for calming angry customers (listed on page 26)? See how many you can write down from memory.

1. _____

2. _____

3. _____

4. _____

Can you recall the five rules for better customer service (listed on page 31)? Write down as many as you can without looking back.

1. _____

2. _____

3. _____

4. _____

5. _____

S K I L L   L E V E L   A S S E S S M E N T   I I

Based on what you've learned in Session 2, again rate yourself on the following statements. When you are finished, compare your total score to the one you earned at the beginning of this session.

WEAK   **AVERAGE**   **STRONG**

1–4 points   5–7 points   8–10 points

Show ability to cool down angry customers.   _____

Find out what a complaining customer wants.   _____

Ask for details of a complaint; get the story straight.   _____

Apologize to a customer even when it's not your own fault.   _____

Deal well with obstinate customers.   _____

Know what to do when customers become angry.   _____

Handle complaints and criticisms directed at you.   _____

Have a knack for dealing with complaints.   _____

Show ability to turn dissatisfied customers into satisfied ones.   _____

Attend to customers' problems quickly.   _____

Work to develop win-win solutions for customers and clients.   _____

Follow up with customers after resolving complaints.   _____

TOTAL RATING _____

WEAK   **FAIR**   **GOOD**   **STRONG**

Under 48   49–65   66–84   85–120

ACTION PLAN

Many of the skills discussed are interrelated, and building from your strengths is a good place to start improving your overall abilities. But you can't afford to overlook your weaknesses either. List below your three best scores (your **strengths**) and your three lowest scores (your **weaknesses**) from the ratings on the previous page.

STRENGTHS

1._____

2._____

3._____

WEAKNESSES

1._____

2._____

3._____

Comparing the two lists, can you see any ways in which you can use your strengths to improve your weaknesses? If so, write them down briefly.

_____

_____

_____

Now re-examine your three biggest weaknesses. Since it's best to work on them one at a time, list them in this order: Start with the one you think will be the easiest to improve upon, followed by a more difficult one, and then the most difficult one. Next to each, set a timetable for concentrating on them (one week, two weeks, etc.).

TIMETABLE FOR WORKING ON WEAKNESSES/IMPROVEMENT

1. _____

2. _____

3. _____

Using the ideas and information from this session, list at least one technique you can practice to improve each weakness. Also add any ideas of your own.

1. _____

2. _____

3. _____

If you cannot determine a technique or course of action you think will be effective, talk to your supervisor for ideas that can be applied to your specific situation.

At the end of the timeframe you set for improvement on *all* of your weaknesses, look again at the skill level rating on page 34. Rate yourself once more on *all* of the statements listed. You will probably find improvement not only in your weak areas but in the others as well.

S U M M A R Y

The key point to remember when dealing with angry customers is probably the most difficult one to effectively absorb. And that is, *"Remember that the customer is not mad at you personally."* When someone is screaming or sneering at you, it's awfully hard not to take it personally.

With work and with time, however, you can develop a professional detachment from the verbal onslaughts you experience. Not a cynicism, nor a repressed anger, but an attitude that accepts this as part of the challenge of your job.

There are few more rewarding moments for a customer service professional than those occasions when an initially angry customer turns into a well-pleased, appreciative one as a result of your efforts. The tips, techniques, case studies, skill assessments, and action plan in this session will help you to become the type of professional who can accomplish this consistently.

In the next session we'll be taking a look at tough customers in more specific situations, namely, face to face and on the phone. If you think you now have a better understanding of how to calm angry customers and solve problems, it's time to move ahead.

3

FACE TO FACE
AND ON THE PHONE

INTRODUCTION

Not only do tough customers come in all shapes and sizes but they also present themselves in different situations as well. The general techniques we've already covered for handling them still apply, but specialized settings call for specialized solutions.

In this session we're going to break the problem solving down into two broad categories: dealing with customers in person — or face to face — and dealing with them over the telephone. There are characteristics unique to each, and common problem situations unique to each too.

Using what you've already learned as background, you'll discover some specific methods for dealing successfully with a variety of person-to-person and telephone dilemmas that many of you will probably find familiar from your own experiences. These are not all problems involving customer complaints. But they are sensitive and often tricky situations that could escalate into complaints if not handled skillfully.

Here are the topics for Session 3:

Skill Level Assessment I First, let's get an idea of where you think you stand now on some specific skills needed for those face-to-face and telephone encounters.

Juggling More Than One Customer at a Time Perhaps the trickiest — and one of the most common — problems to resolve is when two customers want your attention at the same time. Is there any way to please both of them? At the same time? Find out.

Case Study: Double Trouble Using your experience, imagination — and what you've just learned — let's see what you would do when faced with dual customers dueling for your attention.

Warning Signs of Dissatisfied Customers They're not *saying* they are growing disinterested, frustrated, or angry, but they are giving off nonverbal cues that their patience is just about at an end. Do you know what to look for?

Building Conversational Bridges The client is a very nice person and all but when you showed your interest you didn't expect to get a complete life history. It doesn't seem like the person will ever stop talking, your time is limited, and you've got other customers waiting. How do you get down to business without being rude and turning off the client?

Careful Complaints How careful are you when you take a telephone complaint? Here's how to find out.

Tips on Keeping Conversations Short and Sweet The phone caller has a different way of tying up your time than the customer does in person. But for you, the problem is the same. Here's how to handle long-winded callers.

Five Steps to Solving Caller Problems A step-by-step procedure for ensuring that you thoroughly and effectively handle a caller's complaint.

Case Study: The Lost Payment Here's a way to practice solving caller problems, and to use your own ideas too.

Negotiation by Phone Sometimes you have to play diplomat. Here's how to develop a win-win solution for you and your customer.

Handling Irate Callers How good are you at appeasing unhappy customers by phone? Take this test and find out.

As in all the sessions our **ANSWERS SECTION** and **DO YOU REMEMBER?** page will help you rethink and recall the information presented in this session. Then it's time again for a ....

Skill Level Assessment II Are your skills any sharper than they were 20 minutes ago? Learn any new ones?

Action Plan Here's how to sort out your strong points and weak ones — and a plan for turning those weaknesses into strengths.

Now let's take a look at some of those personal encounters of the worst kind — and also see if those voices on the other end of the line are problem people or people with problems. Here's Session 3: *Face to Face and On the Phone.*

S K I L L   L E V E L   A S S E S S M E N T   I

Using the chart below, rate your own skills as they relate to the following statements:

WEAK	**AVERAGE**	**STRONG**
1–4 points	5–7 points	8–10 points

When facing customers, can tell when they're dissatisfied
even when nothing is said. _____

Able to handle more than one customer at a time. _____

Know how to deal with customers who talk on and on. _____

Know how to deal with customers <u>on</u> the <u>phone</u> who talk incessantly. _____

Know how to turn a conversation back to business. _____

Handle complaints carefully; get all facts correct. _____

Able to solve problems on the telephone. _____

Know how to turn a phone conversation back to business. _____

Able to deal successfully with irate phone callers. _____

Able to negotiate with an angry customer. _____

Know how to find negotiating options. _____

Find alternative solutions for customer problems. _____

TOTAL RATING _____

WEAK	**FAIR**	**GOOD**	**STRONG**
Under 48	49–65	66–84	85–120

A score under 65 means there's room for improvement.
A score between 66–84 shows you're doing well but can
do better. Any score over 85 means it's just a matter of
building on your strengths.

JUGGLING MORE THAN ONE CUSTOMER AT A TIME

Two customers approach you at once. Who do you help first? Here's a possible scenario dealing with just that problem, and some tips on handling it.

A woman and a man who don't know each other approach you at the same time. Both appear to be in a hurry and want different things. The man asks for something but before you can reply the woman demands to be waited on first.

Don't get flustered. Smile and tell the woman, "What you want is right over there." Then wait on the man. Excuse yourself as soon as possible and go back to the woman, who is probably looking at the display you pointed out to her. Discuss some points of the merchandise with her, then **find a reason to excuse yourself** and say, "I'll be right back." Use the same tactic with the man. Take care of both people in this way until both are satisfied.

If both customers happen to be interested in the same merchandise, try waiting on both together by talking to a two-person audience. One person may just influence the other, and with any luck you can make two sales. Just be sure to give them equal attention.

Using your own work or type of business as a background, think of statements you could make to give a reason to excuse yourself as mentioned above. Here's an example:

"Why don't you think about which item you like best for a minute? I'll be right back."

What else could you say?

1. _____

2. _____

3. _____

CASE #1: DOUBLE TROUBLE

Catherine is working at a clothing store when two customers approach her simultaneously.

Man: *Hi, I need a few ties that'll go with a charcoal pin-striped suit I have. Could you help me pick out a couple real quick?*

Woman: *Excuse me, I'm in something of a rush and I need a dress shirt for my husband, size 16–33. Not a white one though. Could you show me what you have?*

What does Catherine do? What would you do?

Assume that the dress shirts are near where you're standing and that the ties are four counters over. Write down what you'd say first, then what you would do.

You say:

_____

_____

What you would do next:

_____

_____

Now you're on your own. Assume you're juggling the two customers as described above. Write down your actions and statements to each customer in turn. Include what you think would be their likely responses to each of your statements.

_____

_____

_____

_____

_____

_____

_____

_____

_____

_____

WATCH FOR WARNING SIGNS

A customer who is dissatisfied may not say a word even though his or her body language is screaming volumes. Be on the lookout for these visual warning signs. They are good indicators that the customer is about to walk out on you.

1. Loss of eye contact. If a customer averts his or her eyes and won't meet your gaze, he or she may have written you off.

2. Change in tone of voice. An angry voice is an obvious clue. A more subtle signal might be abrupt or hurried responses to you.

3. Uncomfortable body movements. If your customer keeps shifting his weight or crossing and uncrossing arms, it could be a sign of irritation.

Look for these signs the next time you suspect a customer is unhappy with your service. And keep these three warning signs in mind for later.

THE CONVERSATION TRAP

Everyone in customer service knows the value of taking a personal interest in customers. But sometimes that interest comes with a price. Sometimes you can find yourself trapped in a conversation that doesn't relate to the business at hand. The customer talks and talks while others are waiting. And it's not always simple to ease out of these traps gracefully.

Here are three common conversation traps and suggestions for getting back to business — without offending the customer:

1. The chitchat trap. This conversation begins innocently enough — the customer mentions something about his or her personal life. The subject isn't about a service problem, mind you, but about something else — the weather, the cold he or she caught because of it, or an incident that occurred on the way to see you.

Being courteous, you reply with a comment of your own. Whoops! You just gave that person permission to elaborate. And elaborate he does. Meanwhile, you still don't know the reason the customer is there. Cutting off her talk might seem rude or insensitive. Still, it's time to change the subject.

In these situations try the "bridging technique." Keep eye contact and lean forward. When the customer takes a breath at the end of a sentence, slide in a comment of your own. Pick up on the last thing the person said, and use that to bridge to the reason the customer has come to see you. For example, say, "Sounds like you've had a busy day before you ever got here. What can I do for you?"

End your bridging statement with a question. It switches the customer's attention to the business at hand. By using this type of conversational bridge, you can avoid sounding like you're changing the subject abruptly.

2. The interruption trap. If you are frequently interrupted by customers, you may be unconsciously sending "interrupt me" signals. Usually this results from your pausing too long after a sentence, suggesting that you are waiting for a reply.

To escape this trap, adopt a habit of holding onto your "turn" in the conversation by eliminating these pauses between sentences. Also, you can raise your vocal pitch at the end of each sentence.

3. The space invader trap. Some people trap you in conversation by moving into your personal space. Typically, they move in closer to you, you move back a bit, they move in, and so on. And they're usually talking all the while. It's never rude to protect your personal space. There's nothing wrong with establishing a comfortable distance between you and a customer, so simply step away a few paces. If that doesn't solve it try moving behind a desk or counter, if possible.

B U I L D I N G   B R I D G E S

Using what you've just learned about the bridging technique, write down statements you could make to turn a long-winded customer's attention to the business at hand.

1. CUSTOMER: … and I used to work in the food service industry before I retired. Over 40 years in the business and believe me I don't miss it at all. When I think of the constant hassles and the infighting, and the corporate politics — I was a VP by the time I left — I sometimes wonder how I put up with it all.

YOU:_____

_____

2. CUSTOMER: Well, I know a bit about your products and your business from my son. He just graduated from college last year and he's working in the same industry. He went through school on a full scholarship — terrific grades — and had a number of offers right off the bat. Not easy in this economy.

YOU:_____

_____

3. CUSTOMER: Well, we're going on vacation in a couple of weeks. Down to the islands. We haven't really taken any time out in years and, come to think of it, we almost didn't get to go this year because we had so much trouble getting a flight. Seems everyone wants to go there this time of year. But at the last minute we find a travel agent who found a cancellation and we jumped on it. It wasn't that cheap, you understand, a last-minute booking and all but we really want to get away and that was our first choice.

YOU:_____

_____

Examples of bridging statements you could make in these situations are in the **ANSWERS SECTION** on page 49.

ARE YOU A CAREFUL
COMPLAINT TAKER?

No matter how well prepared customer service people are, they are still discomposed by complaints. See how carefully you handle dissatisifed customers. Answer each question below **YES** or **NO**, then score yourself.

	YES	NO
1. Do you ask questions to determine the real cause of a customer's dissatisfaction?	❏	❏
2. Do you listen carefully for details when a customer complains?	❏	❏
3. Do you allow the customer to complain without interrupting?	❏	❏
4. Do you bear in mind how you feel when you are dissatisfied as a customer?	❏	❏
5. Do you have a genuine interest in your customer's satisfaction?	❏	❏
6. Are you friendly, even when faced with a complaining customer?	❏	❏
7. Do you quickly follow through with a solution you promised to a customer?	❏	❏
8. Do you accept the notion that there is always a chance that the customer will complain?	❏	❏
9. Do you check back with customers to make sure problems are solved to their satisfaction?	❏	❏
10. Do you make it apparent that the customer's happiness is your top priority?	❏	❏

Total Number of YES Answers _____

A score of 8–10 **YES** answers indicates that you are on the right track. You probably do a pretty good job at handling complaints. A lower score means that you need to reconsider that a complaint is a chance to keep a customer, not lose one.

QUICK TIPS

Customers who talk incessantly on the telephone can be just as much of a problem as they are in person. And you can't treat these long-winded callers rudely. Here are three ways to keep phone conversations short and sweet but still complete.

1. Start summarizing. Once you can get a word in edgewise, say, "Now let me be certain I have this right …" Then summarize the main points discussed. If the customer voices no disagreement, move on to summarize what action will be taken.

2. Offer to call the customer back. This involves saying something such as, "I think you've described the problem very well and I'd like to get to work on it immediately. But just in case you have something important to add, let me call you back."

If you have already covered the important ground, the customer will realize that a callback from you isn't necessary. Your words have shown an interest in what the customer is saying and have successfully stopped the person from continuing unnecessarily.

3. Grab their attention. Often you can effectively cut off long-winded callers by interrupting them with an attention-getting line such as, "Wait a minute, I think I have an idea! We can take care of this by …" The idea here is for your interruption to sound like it comes from enthusiasm; the caller won't think you are being rude but rather just anxious to help.

Try to remember these three techniques next time a customer talks nonstop about his or her problem.

FIVE STEPS TO SOLVING CALLER PROBLEMS

A successful problem solver is one-part detective, one-part psychologist, and two-parts psychic.

Armed with a high level of curiosity, a genuine interest in helping others — and the following techniques — any customer service phone rep can lay the groundwork for solving caller problems.

1. Dig, dig, dig. Before you can solve a caller's problem, you need the basic information. That means customer name, account number, address, phone number, and the product or service related to the problem. (The last item is key as it may not come up when you pull the customer's file from the computer.)

2. Repeat information to the caller. Say something like, "Let me see if I have all the information …" This gives you a chance to clarify your understanding of the problem and provides the caller a chance to revise anything he or she said.

3. Determine if there is an immediate solution. Every problem isn't a major one. Sometimes just asking the customer what he or she would like you to do will be enough for you to resolve the situation.

4. Create a course of action. Let the customer know specifically what you intend to do.

5. Follow through. Once you've told the customer what you're going to do, be certain you do it and do it as quickly as you possibly can. Otherwise, you're just creating a bigger problem.

C A S E   # 2 :   T H E   L O S T   P A Y M E N T

Your phone rings and a customer is calling with this complaint.

"I just received a notice on the last bill you sent me. It says that you haven't received my payment. And it says you're adding an extra $10 for a late charge. But I mailed that check to you a good week before the due date."

Using the five steps outlined on the previous page, see how quickly (and effectively) you can solve this customer's problem. Write down what you would say or do for each step. (A word of advice: There are actually two problems you'll have to solve here.)

1. Dig, dig, dig.

_____

_____

2. Repeat information to the caller.

_____

_____

3. Determine if there is an immediate solution.

_____

_____

4. Create a course of action.

_____

_____

5. Follow through.

_____

_____

Suggested solutions and statements are in the **ANSWERS SECTION** on page 49.

N E G O T I A T I O N   B Y   P H O N E

Sometimes solving a phone complaint is more complicated than simply correcting a mistake. That's when you need to employ a key skill for success on the telephone — the art of negotiation.

The goal of any negotiation is the same as the goal for successful customer service — arriving at a solution that is acceptable to both the customer and your company, namely, the win-win solution.

Here are some guidelines for putting negotiation to work for you in your next call.

1. Don't attack a customer's position. Look behind it. When customers set forth their positions, neither accept nor reject them. Instead, treat them as possible options. Top-notch negotiating involves sending the message that you have an open mind and that you honestly want to help.

2. Lay the groundwork. Try to establish what the other person needs to strike an agreement. There will often be more than one such need and this will give you more negotiating options.

3. Be open-minded and flexible. One of the main rules about negotiating is that at times there are no rules. You must play the conversation by ear to find the balance between a customer's satisfaction and an outcome you can realistically carry out. Otherwise, you may be anticipating that the customer is holding firm to a position that actually is not written in stone.

4. Always talk with care. There are some key phrases that can help keep tempers cool when negotiating. Use these when appropriate: "Please correct me if I am wrong …" "Let me see if I understand what you're saying." "One fair solution might be …"

5. Ask for a deal. Negotiation is give and take. If you give up something, don't hesitate to ask for something reasonable in return. Always offer alternatives, not ultimatums.

6. Recap your agreement. When you arrive at an agreement, restate your understanding of it. Any discrepancy can then be discussed before another misunderstanding or mistake occurs. You will also make the caller feel more a part of the decision-making process.

HOW WELL DO YOU HANDLE IRATE CALLERS?

The irate caller is a big challenge. But the customer service professional who can satisfy such a caller often wins a customer for life. Here's a test to check your ability to handle those tense calls.

	YES	NO
1. Do you let angry callers tell their whole story without interruption?	❑	❑
2. When irate callers berate you for incompetence do you not take the insult personally?	❑	❑
3. Do you try to repeat the specific complaint of a frustrated customer?	❑	❑
4. Do you ask specifically what clients wish you to do in order to help solve their problems?	❑	❑
5. Do you hold your tongue and keep a calm voice when aggravated callers berate you?	❑	❑
6. Do you use a phrase like "I can see how that would anger you" as a way of diffusing the situation?	❑	❑
7. Do you allow the flustered caller to repeat his or her complaint a few times so that the caller can be sure you understand what's wrong?	❑	❑
8. Do you reassure callers that you will do everything you can to help them?	❑	❑
9. Do you give the caller your name so that he or she has a dependable contact?	❑	❑
10. Do you end your phone conversations with a sincere "thank you" despite the way you've been treated?	❑	❑

Total Number of YES Answers _____

If you scored eight or more **YES** answers, you have the patience of a saint plus the motivation of a peak performer. If you have fewer than eight **YES** answers, you need to take a few moments to become more relaxed and understanding.

Here are some suggested "bridging" statements for each of the three customers described in "Building Bridges."

1. **"It must be nice to be away from all that and have the time to get out and do whatever you want. What brings you here today?"**

2. **"Your son sounds like someone we could use here. What can I do for you?"**

3. **"Sounds like a terrific vacation. Are you looking for something for the trip?"**

Suggested solutions for the "Five Steps to Solving Caller Problems: The Lost Payment."

1. Dig, dig, dig. "Can I have your name and account number? And what's your current address and phone number? And this was your payment for the month of June?"

2. Repeat information to the caller. "So the due date was the 15th and you mailed your check in on the 8th? And you just received an overdue notice with a late charge fee of $10, is that right?"

3. Determine if there is an immediate solution. "Well, I'll be happy to remove the late charge fee from your account, OK?"

Naturally that will be fine with the customer but it solves only half the problem. What happened to her payment?

4. Create a course of action. "Now, as for the payment you sent in, it sounds to me as if it arrived about the same time the late notice went out. Let me do this. I'll check with the accounting department to make sure they received it. Can I call you back on this?"

5. Follow through. "Hi, Mrs. Simmons? I've checked with accounting and they do have your check so there's nothing to worry about. Apparently it was delayed in the mail and, just like I thought, the late notice had already gone out before anyone could stop it. You can just throw it away, alright? Thanks for calling us about this."

List three techniques to keep phone calls short and sweet — even with long-winded customers.

1. _____

2. _____

3. _____

Listed below are the six tips for "Negotiation by Phone." Below each statement, write down why it is important or how it furthers your chances of successfully negotiating a win-win solution.

1. Don't attack a customer's position.

_____

_____

2. Lay the groundwork.

_____

_____

3. Be open-minded and flexible.

_____

_____

4. Always talk with care.

_____

_____

5. Ask for a deal.

_____

_____

6. Recap your agreement.

_____

_____

Based on what you've learned in Session 3, again rate yourself on the following statements. When you are finished, compare your total score to the one you earned at the beginning of this session.

WEAK   **AVERAGE**   **STRONG**

1–4 points   5–7 points   8–10 points

When facing customers, can tell when they're dissatisfied even when nothing is said.   _____

Able to handle more than one customer at a time.   _____

Know how to deal with customers who talk on and on.   _____

Know how to deal with customers on the phone who talk incessantly.   _____

Know how to turn a conversation back to business.   _____

Handle complaints carefully; get all facts correct.   _____

Able to solve problems on the telephone.   _____

Know how to turn a phone conversation back to business.   _____

Able to deal successfully with irate _phone_ callers.   _____

Able to negotiate with an angry customer.   _____

Know how to find negotiating options.   _____

Find alternative solutions for customer problems.   _____

TOTAL RATING _____

WEAK   **FAIR**   **GOOD**   **STRONG**

Under 48   49–65   66–84   85–120

A C T I O N   P L A N

Many of the skills are interrelated, and building from your strengths is a good place to start improving your overall abilities. But you can't afford to overlook your weaknesses either. List below your three best scores (your **strengths**) and your three lowest scores (your **weaknesses**) from the ratings on the previous page.

STRENGTHS

1. _____

2. _____

3. _____

WEAKNESSES

1. _____

2. _____

3. _____

Comparing the two lists, can you see any ways in which you can use your strengths to improve your weaknesses? If so, write them down briefly.

_____

_____

_____

Now re-examine your three biggest weaknesses. Since it's best to work on them one at a time, list them in this order: Start with the one you think will be the easiest to improve upon, followed by a more difficult one, and then the most difficult one.

Next to each, set a timetable for concentrating on them (one week, two weeks, etc.)

T I M E T A B L E   F O R   W O R K I N G   O N   W E A K N E S S E S / I M P R O V E M E N T

1. _____

2. _____

3. _____

Using the ideas and information from this session, list at least one technique you can practice to improve each weakness. Also add any ideas of your own.

1. _____

2. _____

3. _____

If you cannot determine a technique or course of action you think will be effective, talk to your supervisor for ideas that can be applied to your specific situation.

At the end of the time frame you set for improvement on *all* of your weaknesses, look again at the skill level rating on page 51. Rate yourself once more on *all* of the statements listed. You will probably find improvement not only in your weak areas but in the others as well.

S U M M A R Y

The customer service skills we've examined in this session are designed to apply to a variety of different, and fairly specific, situations. The problems you will face in your own business or service will, of course, vary according to the nature of that business or service industry. But if you look at the situations closely, it should be easy to see problems you encounter that parallel some of the ones presented in this session.

Skills such as dealing with more than one customer at a time, recognizing when a customer is growing annoyed, negotiating with a client or customer, and all of the others discussed in this session, are valuable to have at your disposal regardless of the type of customer service work you do.

In Session 4 we'll be going back to more generalized situations again … but with a twist. We're going to consider what to do when confronted by tough customers who are wrong — customers whose complaints stem from their own actions or misunderstandings. We'll also take a good, long look at what you can do when that most dreaded of all occasions arises: when you are the one who's made the mistake.

EVERYBODY MAKES MISTAKES
(CAN THIS CUSTOMER BE SAVED?)

INTRODUCTION

Yes, everybody makes mistakes. You. Your co-workers. Your boss. The customers. Everybody.

But not everyone, particularly complaining customers, can own up to them. Rarer still is the customer service professional who can and does turn his or her own mistake into a success, making the customer relationship stronger than it would have been had the mistake not happened.

Whether it's you who are wrong or the customer who is wrong, the first priority is to correct the error — assuming it's correctable. The larger, looming question, however, is this: Can this customer be saved? Can the customer still be satisfied; can he or she be kept as a customer of your business or service in spite of the error? Can you win back their good will?

We're going to be dealing with these questions next and here is what's in store for you in Session 4:

Skill Level Assessment I   What skills do you need to correct mistakes? Which ones do you have?

Believe It or Not: Mistakes Can Actually Help You   You really can perform the customer service equivalent of spinning straw into gold — if you have the know-how. And here it is.

Case Study: The Monday Morning Headache   Making a blunder is bad enough. Discovering it on a Monday morning is worse yet. Here's a practice session for handling an error and hopefully saving a week.

The Good News About Goof-Ups   To err is human, but will clients and customers really forgive? Find out.

The Big Three Questions Customers Ask After a Mistake When a blunder goes down, customers want to know the whys and wherefores. But be careful what you say. A real disaster could be in the details.

How Well Do You Keep Commitments? Keeping your commitments means never having to say you're sorry. It's also a good way to avoid making mistakes. How well do you keep your commitments? Here's a test that will tell you.

The Customer Is Not Always that Right! Customer service blasphemy? Treason? Have we gone mad? Not at all. Read on.

When a Customer Is Dishonest Not all clients and customers are paragons of virtue. How do you handle one who lies?

Case Study: A Matter of Truth Here's a very tough situation with a difficult decision to make. There may be no right or wrong answer, but it'll give you a chance to consider what you would do if you're unsure of your customer's motives.

When a "Wrong" Customer Calls That complaining customer is probably in the wrong on this one. But are you combative or compassionate? Can you swallow your pride and turn them into a repeat customer?

The **ANSWERS SECTION** and **DO YOU REMEMBER?** quizzes will round out the session followed by:

Skill Level Assessment II Our quantitative remeasurement to figure out how you're doing.

Action Plan Time to evaluate your strong points and weak ones — and to develop a plan for turning those weaknesses into strengths.

No one likes to make mistakes. But not everyone can correct them successfully or turn them to their advantage. You have the opportunity to do both if you master the information and apply the skills we'll be showing you in Session 4: *Everybody Makes Mistakes (Can This Customer Be Saved?)*.

SKILL LEVEL ASSESSMENT I

Using the chart below, rate your own skills as they relate to the following statements:

WEAK	**AVERAGE**	**STRONG**
1–4 points	5–7 points	8–10 points

Able to recover from mistakes you've made. _____

Know how to handle a customer after you've made a mistake. _____

Take steps to prevent errors from recurring. _____

Can regain customer's confidence after your error. _____

Good at keeping business commitments. _____

Know how to profit from your own mistakes. _____

Handle angry customers well, even when they are wrong. _____

Can make customers see their mistakes without antagonizing them. _____

Able to recognize when a customer is lying. _____

Able to deal with a customer who is lying. _____

Know how to tell a customer that he or she is mistaken. _____

Apologize to a customer for a mistake. _____

TOTAL RATING _____

WEAK	**FAIR**	**GOOD**	**STRONG**
Under 48	49–65	66–84	85–120

A score under 65 means there's room for improvement. A score between 66–84 shows you're doing well but can do better. Any score over 85 means it's just a matter of building on your strengths.

BELIEVE IT OR NOT:
MISTAKES CAN ACTUALLY HELP YOU

Everyone makes mistakes. If you think about it, you've probably made your share of them over the years — a misdirected package, a misrouted file, a forgotten deadline. Typical reactions? Embarrassment, anger, and frustration.

There is great virtue in making mistakes, in learning from them, and in improving along the way. Why don't people realize that mistakes are really great opportunities? When you fix a problem, you not only get a chance to right a wrong but you can build a strong working relationship too.

Not only can you recover from your blunders but you can use them to turn yourself into a winner as well. Here's how:

1. Make things right. Your first responsibility is to correct the mistake. The faster you address the problem, the more credible you'll appear to others.

2. Apologize. When you make a mistake, you'll usually gain stature by apologizing in a direct way. You won't appear incompetent, only human. And you send the message that you're big enough to admit it.

3. Let the matter rest. There is no need to beat a dead horse by bringing the matter up over and over again. One apology suffices.

4. Learn more about operations. If you have to track down a goof, use the occasion to learn more about the intricacies of your company's business. This knowledge will come in handy over time and can prevent mistakes down the line.

5. Ask if you can do something else. After resolving your mistake, ask if you can help in any other way. Offering something extra can build goodwill.

6. Follow up after you've resolved the problem. Check up to see how things are going. After all, you want to make sure your mistake has caused no more fallout. You'll boost your reputation for being responsive, concerned, and proactive.

7. Let others know you've learned something. Assure those affected by your error that it won't happen again. In fact, they may come to you the next time a similar problem comes up.

Bob Dalton walked into his office Monday morning and picked up where he'd left off the previous week. He had taken a frantic call late Friday from a customer who needed a delivery made on Wednesday. Bob had assured him it would be no problem and now he wanted to get the paperwork in place and the order rolling.

Checking schedules, Bob suddenly feels a migraine coming on. In the late Friday afternoon rush, he had forgotten that the routes on the delivery schedules were being changed, effective today. His customer's normal Wednesday delivery is now made on Mondays. It will be a week from today before his customer can receive his delivery.

What Would You Do?

Assume you're Bob and write down what you would do next. Remember that getting the delivery to the customer on time is not an option open to you. Your problem now is one of customer relations.

_____

_____

_____

_____

_____

_____

_____

_____

_____

Five suggested steps for handling this problem are listed in the **ANSWERS SECTION** at the end of this session. Check to see how many of them you incorporated into your course of action.

There's been a major error on a client's account and it was your fault. Is there any chance of regaining your customer's faith in you?

The good news is, in the overwhelming majority of cases, clients forgive even when the worst happens — provided you do three things:

1. Be honest. Tell the client exactly what happened and don't try to minimize what went wrong. Most importantly, don't try to cover up or make excuses. A straightforward explanation will give you credibility with your client — essential in rebuilding a good relationship.

2. Learn what went wrong and implement change. Once you've found out what went wrong, take steps to prevent that error from happening again. And then tell your client what you've done as a result of the error.

3. Don't let it happen again. You can win a client back after a mistake. But if the same mistake recurs, he or she may very well write you off as incompetent.

Using your own experience, think of a mistake or error you made that caused a problem for a customer or client. Describe it briefly.

_____

_____

_____

_____

Using the three steps outlined above as guidelines, describe what you did or didn't do for each of those steps. Then, with the benefit of hindsight, describe what you could have done or would do if a similar situation occurred in the future.

1. What you did or didn't do: Be honest.

_____

_____

What you could do in a similar situation:

_____

_____

2. Learn what went wrong and implement change. What you did or didn't do:

_____

_____

What you could do in a similar situation:

_____

_____

3. Don't let it happen again. What you did or didn't do.

_____

_____

What you could do in a similar situation:

_____

_____

THE BIG THREE QUESTIONS CUSTOMERS ASK AFTER A MISTAKE

When a mistake happens, customers want to know three things:

1. **How did it happen?**

2. **Who made it happen?**

3. **Why did it happen?**

The answer to one of these questions — and only one — is crucial. Which is it and why is it crucial?

_____

_____

The correct answer is in the **ANSWERS SECTION** on page 67.

HOW WELL DO YOU KEEP COMMITMENTS?

One of the keys to avoiding mistakes is keeping your commitments — to yourself, your employer, and your customer. How well do you keep commitments? This quiz will tell you. Check your rating when you've finished.

1. I _____ assign deadlines to the commitments I make.

   A. Usually   B. Sometimes   C. Rarely

2. I _____ put my major commitments in writing so I can monitor myself.

   A. Usually   B. Sometimes   C. Rarely

3. When I find I can't keep an earlier commitment, I _____.

   A. Panic   B. Keep quiet   C. Explain why

4. If I have any doubt about being able to make a commitment, I _____.

   A. Don't make it   B. Stall   C. Change the subject

5. Before making a commitment to a customer, I always _____.

   A. Think it through   B. Leave myself an out   C. Get my boss to approve it

6. I _____ take commitments seriously.

   A. Always   B. Sometimes   C. Rarely

7. What happens when you're unable to keep a commitment? _____

   A. Nothing   B. I always learn something   C. I blame others

8. What kind of commitments do you like to make? _____

   A. Easy ones   B. Ones I feel I can meet   C. Ones I can get out of if necessary

9. When you fail to keep a promise, do you offer something in return? _____

   A. Usually   B. Sometimes   C. Rarely

10. Do you feel miserable when you can't keep a promise? _____

    A. Usually   B. Sometimes   C. Rarely

Give yourself one point for each of the following answers you selected:

1 - A; 2 - A; 3 - C; 4 - A; 5 - A; 6 - A; 7 - B; 8 - B; 9 - A; 10 - A. In addition, you can earn half-points for the following selected answers: **3 - B; 4 - C; 5 - B; 8 - A.** A score of 8-10 means you're excellent at making and meeting commitments, 6½ to 7½ is good, 6 is average, and anything below 5½ is unsatisfactory.

THE CUSTOMER IS *NOT* ALWAYS RIGHT!

There. We've said it.

Despite everything you've learned in training for your job, despite everything you've always heard, the fact of the matter is: Customers aren't always right.

Dogmatically adhering to the principle that "the customer is always right" can actually prevent you from identifying and solving customer problems.

But when customers are in the wrong, it takes tact and diplomacy to deal with them without blaming, embarrassing, alienating, or angering them. After all, you still want to keep their business. And it's still your job to help them through the problem.

Here are some options for those times when the customer is wrong.

Play pretend. Pretend that the customer is right. This will soothe him or her and at least prevent the angry from growing angrier. Playing pretend is easy enough to do but it can cost to keep a customer happy so you may want to use this option sparingly.

Keep it positive. When a customer is wrong, try to keep a positive slant in telling him or her "no." After expressing your refusal, let the customer know you sincerely regret that you can't do more. ("I'm really sorry but that's all I can do.")

Tell it like it is. You'll have to muster up plenty of diplomacy for this one. You'll also have to have a very thorough knowledge of the product or service in question. The trick here is to explain everything in such a manner that the customer will draw his or her own conclusion — that conclusion being that he or she made the mistake.

Try to keep these three options in mind the next time you're confronted with a customer who is in the wrong.

For those times when you do decide to "tell it like it is" you are, in effect, correcting the customer. Try using these four strategies to make the job easier.

1. Hear them out. Make sure your customer feels you have listened to the whole story. Otherwise, he or she might become defensive.

2. Keep the correction private. There's no sense in addressing the matter in front of others because embarrassment is guaranteed. Also, you're smart to drop the matter immediately — don't mention it to them again.

3. Help the customer save face. Find something the customer has done correctly. Express understanding about how a mistake could have been made. This gives the customer an "out."

4. Provide reassurance. Make it clear that you know your customer is smart and competent. Minimize the mistake to reduce its importance.

Read the scenario below and then write down what you would say and do to resolve it, using some of the strategies and options we've just covered.

You are a customer service person in a large self-service store. A man approaches with a large cardboard box that contains a bookcase he purchased. He complains that when he tried to assemble it he discovered that the bookcase was defective. He loudly states that he wants a replacement or a refund.

You remove the pieces of the bookcase from the box. It is completely ruined. Pulling out the assembly manual you notice that it is only eight-pages long with clear and simple instructions accompanied by a diagram for each step. You ask the customer if the instructions were too complicated but he simply shrugs and repeats that the bookcase was defective. You can see very large cracks and indentations in the wood, as if it has been hammered.

It is obvious to you that the customer did not bother to read the instructions and that the damage to the bookcase was his own fault. (The assembly instructions did not require the use of a hammer.) You have the authority to replace the bookcase but are fairly certain he will ruin that one too. You can give him a refund but that doesn't seem right since the bookcase was not defective. Also, your company's policy is to do all it can to attract repeat customers.

What do you do?

_____

_____

_____

_____

_____

_____

_____

_____

W H E N   A   C U S T O M E R   I S   D I S H O N E S T

In rare instances you will come across a client or customer who will try to pull a fast one in order to get something for nothing — in other words, a customer who is lying.

You'll have to have your radar on for this one. Sometimes the story he or she gives just doesn't seem right. Sometimes their demands seem a bit exorbitant. Other times it's something in their look or the sound of their voice that raises the alarm.

Here's a situation where prudence comes into play. If the customer or client has a history with your company, check his or her file. If it's a long-standing customer, give that person the benefit of the doubt. Even if this is a case of a fast one being pulled, the repeat business may be worth it. If a similar incident has occurred before, however, check with your supervisor.

If the request comes from a small-volume or one-time customer, stick by the company rules regarding return policy. While pleasing the customer is important, there has to be a point at which you stick to your guns. If the company goes under because of sky-high expenses, there won't be any customers to please. Or paychecks either.

CASE #2: A MATTER OF TRUTH

Jennifer was puzzled. The software package — a compilation of demographic databases of potential customers — that her client claimed was defective had not yet been returned.

The client, Rod, had called her a week ago complaining about it. She had offered to send him a replacement as soon as he sent back the original. The information in the database was exclusive to her company and the packages sold for $20,000 each. The problem could be that Rod simply didn't know how to run it — it was rather complicated — but she couldn't risk leaving a working one out there.

Rod had said he'd send it out the next day but as yet it hadn't arrived. Now here was a message on her voicemail with him screaming that he needed the replacement sent immediately via overnight service, and that he had sent the original back to Jennifer last week and that if she didn't have it, it must still be in the mail. But why would he send something so valuable by ordinary mail?

Rod had done business with Jennifer's company for years and there had been no problems. He was a valued customer. She couldn't just tell him it was company policy not to send a replacement and let it go at that. And what if the original really was defective?

But hadn't she heard a rumor somewhere that his small business was in trouble? Could he really be thinking of getting another copy of the database for free — and selling it on his own to raise some cash? That didn't seem possible.

What would you do if you were Jennifer? What would you say when you talked to Rod?

_____

_____

_____

_____

WHEN A "WRONG" CUSTOMER CALLS: COMBAT OR COMPASSION?

When customers call with complaints, they are always certain they are right. But sometimes they're wrong — and it's hard to tell them that. Here's a short quiz to see how well you handle such customers. Answer **YES** or **NO** to each question and tally your score at the end.

	YES	NO
1. Do you let the caller tell the whole story without interruption?	❏	❏
2. Do you restate the complaint in your own words?	❏	❏
3. Do you remember to ask specifically what your caller wishes you to do to correct the problem?	❏	❏
4. Do you immediately apologize for any inconvenience?	❏	❏
5. Do you ask your caller to point out the error when you are not able to see it?	❏	❏
6. Do you allow your caller to tell the same story two or three times without frustration on your part?	❏	❏
7. Do you always look for a way to prove your customers are right even when they are not?	❏	❏
8. Do you refrain from specifically pointing out where a customer has gone wrong?	❏	❏
9. Do you give the caller enough time to figure out where he or she has made an error?	❏	❏
10. Do you always end such conversations on an upbeat, friendly tone?	❏	❏

Total Number of YES Answers _____

A perfect 10 **YES** answers shows your ability to turn even the most irascible client into a repeat customer. Score 8–10, and you know your stuff, but you can do better. Fewer than eight **YES** answers indicates that you may be too willing to do combat with your clients.

Suggested course of action to the problem in Case #1: The Monday Morning Headache.

1. **Immediately call and explain what happened.**

2. **Apologize and accept the blame.**

3. **Outline what can be done to rectify the problem. (Perhaps a special delivery can be made Thursday or Friday — still late but better than the customer waiting for a week.)**

4. **Send some tangible token of apology such as a personal letter.**

5. **Explain what steps you'll take to make sure the error doesn't happen again.**

ANSWER FOR QUICK TIPS QUESTION

The correct answer is #3, "Why did it happen?"

Question #1, "How did it happen?" is important only as it provides information about #3. It is a recap of the steps that led to the error.

Question #2, "Who made it happen?" is almost always asked but simply placing blame for an error will not help correct it (unless it relates to #3) and is often counterproductive.

Question #3, "Why did it happen?" is the crucial question because the answer to it provides the means for making certain the error is not repeated. Once the reasons for the error are known, safeguards can be put in place to prevent its recurrence.

DO YOU REMEMBER?

List three approaches you can take when "The Customer Is *Not* Always Right."

1. _____

2. _____

3. _____

Can you recall the four strategies to use when you must correct a customer?

1. _____

2. _____

3. _____

4. _____

In "Believe It or Not: Mistakes Can Actually Help You," we listed seven ways in which a mistake can be turned into a positive for you and your career. How many can you recall?

1. _____

2. _____

3. _____

4. _____

5. _____

6. _____

7. _____

S K I L L   L E V E L   A S S E S S M E N T   I I

Based on what you've learned in session 4, again rate yourself on the following statements. When you are finished, compare your total score to the one you earned at the beginning of this session.

WEAK   **AVERAGE**   **STRONG**

1–4 points   5–7 points   8–10 points

Able to recover from mistakes you've made.   _____

Know how to handle a customer after you've made a mistake.   _____

Take steps to prevent errors from recurring.   _____

Can regain customer's confidence after your error.   _____

Good at keeping business commitments.   _____

Know how to profit from your own mistakes.   _____

Handle angry customers well, even when they are wrong.   _____

Can make customers see their mistakes without antagonizing them.   _____

Able to recognize when a customer is lying.   _____

Able to deal with a customer who is lying.   _____

Know how to tell a customer that he or she is mistaken.   _____

Apologize to a customer for a mistake.   _____

                                              TOTAL RATING _____

WEAK	FAIR	GOOD	STRONG
Under 48	49–65	66–84	85–120

A C T I O N   P L A N

Many of the skills are interrelated, and building from your strengths is a good place to start improving your overall abilities. But you can't afford to overlook your weaknesses either. List below your three best scores (your **strengths**) and your three lowest scores (your **weaknesses**) from the ratings above.

STRENGTHS   **WEAKNESSES**

1._____   1. _____

2._____   2. _____

3._____   3. _____

Comparing the two lists, can you see any ways in which you can use your strengths to improve your weaknesses? If so, write them down briefly.

_____

_____

_____

Now re-examine your three biggest weaknesses. Since it's best to work on them one at a time, list them in this order: Start with the one you think will be the easiest to improve upon, followed by a more difficult one, and then the most difficult one. Next to each, set a timetable for concentrating on them (one week, two weeks, etc.).

TIMETABLE FOR WORKING ON WEAKNESSES/IMPROVEMENT

1. _____

2. _____

3. _____

Using the ideas and information from this session, list at least one technique you can practice to improve each weakness. Also add any ideas of your own.

1. _____

2. _____

3. _____

If you cannot determine a technique or course of action you think will be effective, talk to your supervisor for ideas that can be applied to your specific situation.

At the end of the time frame you set for improvement on *all* of your weaknesses, look again at the skill level rating on page 69. Rate yourself once more on *all* of the statements listed. You will probably find improvement not only in your weak areas but in the others as well.

S U M M A R Y

Among all the skills we've discussed in Session 4, the most important one to helping your career is to take the proper steps to ensure that your mistake doesn't happen again. Take it as a given that you, and everyone else, will make a blunder from time to time. Whether small or serious, that blunder can be overcome, as we've just shown you. And customers and clients understand this, especially when you have handled the aftermath of the error as well as can possibly be expected. After all, they make mistakes too.

What can really destroy your credibility with a client, perhaps irretrievably, is repeating the mistake. This shows that you have not learned from your error, and will raise doubts about your competence in the minds of your customers. To avoid repeating a mistake, pay particular attention to the tips and suggestions included in this session, then take the actions appropriate to your situation. What you will be doing is preparing yourself to *not* do something — in much the same way you would prepare yourself to accomplish some goal by developing a particular skill.

In the next session we're going to go right to the source of customer complaints. Since the easiest problem is the one that never arises, we're going to concentrate on how to prevent problems from ever coming up in the first place.

5

PREVENTING CUSTOMER PROBLEMS

INTRODUCTION

"An ounce of prevention is worth a pound of cure," goes the old adage, and nowhere is that more true than in the area of customer service. Every customer problem you can prevent means one less complaint, one less angry customer, and one less headache for you. There is simply no substitute for customer problem prevention.

You'll notice we emphasize *customer* problem prevention. That's because a problem often comes in two parts. You can't prevent a product from breaking, for example, any more than you can prevent a major storm from causing a missed delivery. Some things are beyond your control.

But the problem itself is only the first part. It's the trigger. Your problem, the real problem, is the customer's reaction to that trigger. And you can very often short circuit a negative reaction before it begins. Preventing a problem with a product or service from escalating until it creates an angry customer — and showing just how long-lasting and damaging the effects are from bad customer experiences — is the focus of this session. Here's what we'll be looking at:

How to Create Problems and Drive Customers Away   The first step in preventing customer problems is — logically enough — preventing yourself from creating any more. But you don't create customer problems, you say? Don't bet on it. Here are some absolutely guaranteed ways for creating problems and driving customers away. And they are things that most all of us are guilty of at one time or another.

Past Problems Make Customers Skeptical   It's much easier to get someone to form an opinion than to change one. Here's some of the customer fallout from bad experiences and what you can do to deal with it.

Case Study: The Shadow of the Past   Here's a minor mystery to sharpen your problem-solving skills.

Three Tips for Problem Prevention A few simple techniques for minimizing those customer service problems.

Prevention: Key to Top-Notch Service How good are you at recognizing the secrets to first-rate prevention? At putting them into practice? Take this test and find out.

When Things Go Wrong With Your Service Here's a procedure that every customer service professional should know. These steps to preventing a problem from becoming a *customer* problem are simple, but not always easy to follow. The results they can bring are well worth the extra effort.

Case Study: The Delayed Driveway By all rights, this customer should have been kicking, screaming, and furious for years. It never happened, owing to the customer service efforts of a true professional. How did he do it? See if you can figure it out.

The Customer Is a Person Too A final look at your own attitudes toward the people who, after all, keep you in business.

Our **ANSWERS SECTION** and **DO YOU REMEMBER?** questions will be a little more extensive in this session. We're going to be posing quite a few problems and asking you to think them through.

Skill Assessment II Our session-ending reassessment of what you've discovered about yourself.

Action Plan A measurement of your strong points and weak ones, and an action plan for turning your weaknesses into strengths.

Ever wish you could make all your problems magically disappear? You can't. But here's how to stop a great many of them from ever happening. It's Session 5: *Preventing Customer Problems.*

S K I L L   L E V E L   A S S E S S M E N T   I

Using the chart below, rate your own skills as they relate to the following statements:

WEAK	AVERAGE	STRONG
1–4 points	5–7 points	8–10 points

Avoid making statements that create customer problems. _____

Able to overcome customer skepticism. _____

Represent product or service accurately. _____

Know steps to prevent problems before they occur. _____

Keep in touch with clients during a problem situation. _____

Treat customers as individuals. _____

Able to win back customers who have had a bad experience with your company or its product or service. _____

Know how to prevent customers from complaining of high costs. _____

Able to spot potential problems before they occur. _____

Prevent a product or service problem from escalating. _____

Take responsibility for customer problems. _____

Able to think of a customer as a partner. _____

TOTAL RATING _____

WEAK	FAIR	GOOD	STRONG
Under 48	49–65	66–84	85–120

A score under 65 means there's room for improvement. A score between 66–84 shows you're doing well but can do better. Any score over 85 means it's just a matter of building on your strengths.

HOW TO CREATE PROBLEMS
AND DRIVE CUSTOMERS AWAY

The prevention of customer problems begins with you. Below are some commonly heard statements that, according to Ron Meiss of Fred Pryor Seminars on "How to Build and Improve Customer Service," are guaranteed to drive your customers away.

In other words, these are statements to avoid at all costs — yet many a customer service professional has used more than one of them more than once.

1. **I don't have anything to do with your problem.**

2. **He's busy — would you call back?**

3. **I have a customer — can you call back?**

4. **There's nothing I can do about it — it's company policy.**

5. **We might have it but I don't have time to check our stock — just come in the store and I'll check for you then.**

6. **We're getting ready to close — would you call back in the morning?**

7. **I just came in — could you call back in about 15 to 20 minutes?**

8. **You'll *have* to give me your account number before I can help you.**

Look these statements over and count how many of them you have used recently. Write down the number.

Can you think of any more statements — commonly used in your business or service — that you would also do well to avoid? Write them down and do your best to never use them again.

_____

_____

_____

_____

PAST PROBLEMS MAKE
A CUSTOMER SKEPTICAL

Once a customer has had a bad experience with your company — or even a recent bad experience with the billing, credit, or shipping department of a similar company — his or her confidence in your ability to deliver is understandably shaken. Sometimes you can sense the mental reservations that are causing your word to be doubted. Here are some typical reasons why customers might be skeptical and actions you can take to overcome that skepticism:

• **Past history.** If you are able to pinpoint the specific event or incident, you may succeed in clearing the air. Don't hesitate to ask questions: "Would you like me to clarify anything?" "Is there something in particular that's concerning you?" "Have I given you all the information you need? "What can I do to convince you?" Don't expect the customer to volunteer information. You must ask.

• **Broken promises.** If there's anything that will shatter customer faith, it's a broken promise — a delivery commitment not fulfilled, a product claim not sustained, an action not taken. The next time you're confronted with a skeptical customer, do a bit of research to determine if a previously broken promise by someone in your organization hasn't shaken the customer's faith.

• **Uncertainty.** Suppose the customer needs information about a product or reassurance regarding a shipping date. If you're unsure of yourself in responding, the customer will probably detect uncertainty in your voice and manner. If you're not absolutely sure of your information or advice, keep it to yourself until you get a concrete answer.

• **Human nature.** Some people are suspicious by nature. They may be insecure, not completely trustworthy themselves, or they might have been burned too many times in the past. No argument or appeal is as convincing as solid proof and irrefutable evidence. Freely offer that to your customers. Do some homework if necessary. It saves a lot of time and energy.

CASE #1: THE SHADOW OF THE PAST

Ann knew her customer wanted to buy the gleaming new oven range she was showing her. The customer's eyes fairly lit up just at the sight of it and Ann had been explaining its features for nearly an hour, all to the customer's growing interest and nods of approval. But every time Ann tried to close the sale the customer seemed to back off — asking question after question about it — most of which Ann had already answered.

Something was holding her back. But what? Finally, she got a clue. After Ann made a favorable mention about the oven's manufacturer, her customer said, "I'm not quite sure about that company." Ann started to reassure the woman about the company's reputation and then caught herself. Thinking quickly, Ann asked her customer a question instead.

What question did Ann ask the customer?

_____

_____

_____

Why did Ann stop herself from extolling the virtues of the oven manufacturer company?

_____

_____

_____

The answers to these questions are in the **ANSWERS SECTION** on page 84. But before you check to see if you've guessed correctly, put yourself in Ann's place and describe what you would say and do to close the sale. Use the pointers about overcoming past customer problems and skepticism as guidelines.

_____

_____

_____

_____

_____

_____

THREE QUICK TIPS
FOR PREVENTING PROBLEMS

1. Avoid the caller Ping-Pong effect. Nothing is more frustrating for callers than to be relayed to the wrong party. Prevent this problem by *letting callers know the name of the person to whom you are transferring their call*. That way, if the call reaches the wrong person, the customer knows who to ask for. Also, give the caller's name to the person you're transferring them to.

2. Stop problems at the point of sale. Cut down on problems and complaints by representing all products and services fairly and accurately. Most problems result from the failure of the product or service to live up to the customer's expectations. Never exaggerate about a product's merits. Make sure the customer knows exactly what to expect.

3. Repair costs? Explain to gain. Perhaps it would cost $25,000 today to completely rebuild a car that in 1980 would have cost $6,018 to buy. But unless customers understand how prices have changed, they won't understand why repairs on your products can seem so costly. The solution? Explain your prices so customers won't feel ripped off when they see the bill later.

Think about your own business or service for a moment. Can you recall any instances where a complaint or problem resulted because one of the procedures above was not followed? Briefly describe the incident.

_____

_____

_____

_____

In retrospect, could that problem or complaint have been avoided if one of these procedures had been utilized? How?

_____

_____

_____

_____

Try to remember these problem-stopping techniques and incorporate them into your own customer service.

PREVENTION: KEY TO TOP-NOTCH SERVICE

Many companies go to admirable lengths to correct an error when it has occurred. Sometimes, though, not enough emphasis is put on preventing the problem. The following quiz can help you determine if you're doing all you can to prevent problems before they occur. Answer each question **YES** or **NO**, then score yourself.

	YES	NO
1. Do you double-check the spelling of a customer's name?	❑	❑
2. Do you verify an account number?	❑	❑
3. Do you ask for a phone number (to call the customer if a question arises later)?	❑	❑
4. Do you repeat the customer's order back to him or her?	❑	❑
5. Do you look for inconsistencies in orders? "All the other items you're ordering are gray. Am I correct that you want this item in blue?"	❑	❑
6. Do you verify your records on the customer? "Mr. Jones, is your mailing address still ...?"	❑	❑
7. Do you check that the items are available?	❑	❑
8. Do you repeat prices to be sure they agree with the customer's understanding?	❑	❑
9. Do you check all quantities ordered?	❑	❑
10. Do you ask for any special instructions on delivery?	❑	❑

Total Number of YES Answers _____

Give yourself a point for every **YES** response; subtract a point for every **NO**. A score of 8–10 is excellent; a score of 7 is good; 6 or fewer means there are many ways in which you could work toward preventing problems. One way to improve your score is to think of each call as a mystery. It's up to you to get all the clues you'll need to solve a problem to the customer's complete satisfaction.

Even the best laid service plans can be derailed by unforeseen circumstances, delays for which you're not responsible, and sheer bad luck. You can't always prevent a problem from occurring with your service, but you can prevent it from creating the additional problem of an irate customer by following some specialized customer service rules.

• **Keep in touch with the customer.** Whether it's a delivery that went awry, a service call that wasn't made, or most any other problem, keeping in touch with the customer is key. The customer will at least know you're concerned and that you're trying. Few things are worse than being kept in the dark, and without word from you about what is going on, a customer will sit and stew until eventually he or she explodes. Then you'll have another problem on your hands.

• **Don't make excuses.** Tell the customers exactly what the problem is.

• **Emphasize your concern.** Let the customer know that *you* know and understand what a hassle this is causing for him or her.

• **Accept the blame — all of it.** Even if what went wrong is not your fault, accept the responsibility. Don't pass the blame off onto others.

• **Soften the blow. Offer extras.** Do anything you can to make up for the customer's inconvenience, even if it costs. If possible offer a discount or some other "freebie."

• **Follow up.** When the service is finally performed, talk to the customer to find out if he or she is satisfied with what was done and if the customer needs anything else done. Check back again in a week or two to make sure everything is still OK.

CASE #2: THE DELAYED DRIVEWAY

The following is a true story.

"This is a routine three-day job," suburban Chicago contractor Rick Hammell assured the customer, who put down a 50 percent deposit for the installation of a new garage door, automatic garage door opener, and short concrete driveway. But "routine" is hardly the word for what actually happened.

A snafu in ordering the correct size door, the overcrowded schedule of a subcontractor hired to pour the concrete, and a spell of inclement weather combined to turn what should have been a short, simple job into a three-week ordeal.

Most customers would have been furious about such a delay, but Rick's client kept calm. Why? What did Rick do?

What would you do?

Using the customer service rules presented in "When Things Go Wrong With Your Service," describe what you would do and say to keep the customer calm. (The actions that Rick successfully took are in the **ANSWERS SECTION**.)

_____

_____

_____

_____

_____

_____

_____

_____

_____

_____

_____

_____

_____

_____

_____

_____

_____

THE CUSTOMER IS A PERSON TOO

It's alarmingly easy to dehumanize clients in customer service work, particularly over the phone. Unless you personalize your service, customer satisfaction is bound to suffer. How well do you relate to clients? Take this quiz and find out.

	YES	NO
1. Do you work around callers' dialects and speech idiosyncracies to get to the message?	❏	❏
2. Do you think of callers and clients as partners rather than adversaries?	❏	❏
3. Are you patient with callers who are hesitant or slow to comprehend?	❏	❏
4. Do you stay relaxed with high-powered customers?	❏	❏
5. Do you create a mental image of callers' faces?	❏	❏
6. Do you allow callers to talk long enough to fully state their concerns?	❏	❏
7. When you've made a point in a discussion with a customer do you wait for a response?	❏	❏
8. Do you talk courteously when conversations become heated and difficult?	❏	❏
9. When callers or customers become quiet, do you try to figure out if their needs are being met?	❏	❏
10. Do you think of callers as real, breathing people — rather than as complaining voices?	❏	❏

Total Number of YES Answers_____

Eight to 10 **YES** answers suggest that you're an expert at treating each client as special. If you scored lower, keep this quiz to remind you that each customer is an individual deserving of your attention and worthy of your concern.

CASE #1: THE SHADOW OF THE PAST

What question did Ann ask her customer?

Have you ever owned an appliance made by this company?

Why did Ann stop herself from extolling the virtues of the manufacturing company?

From the customer's remark, Ann suspected that the woman had once owned a product made by this company and that she had not been happy with it. Ann didn't want to "sell" the woman on the manufacturer until she was sure of whether or not her customer had had a bad experience with them.

CASE #2: THE DELAYED DRIVEWAY

Here is how Rick applied the specialized customer service rules to his situation:

Keep in touch. "I called the customer every day, whether my crew was able to work or not. I wanted him to know that I had not disappeared, and his job was a top priority for me. I encouraged him to call me whenever he wanted an update. I instructed my answering service to page me immediately when this customer called. Even if I was out of town on another job, I called the customer back within 30 minutes."

Don't make excuses. "I was straightforward in explaining the delay, telling the customer precisely what the hold-up was. Customers always appreciate honesty."

Emphasize your concern. "I constantly assured the customer that I knew he was being inconvenienced."

Accept the blame — all of it. "Even though the basic delay was due to the subcontractors, I took full responsibility. I didn't say, 'It's their fault.'"

Soften the blow. Offer extras. "I put up a temporary ramp so that the customer could put his car in the garage in the meantime. I substituted a better-quality door than requested, and poured a longer driveway. I also replaced part of a sidewalk near the garage. Most important, I gave the customer a discount on the total price to make up for the delay."

Follow up. "I made it a point to be there to talk to the customer when the job was finally completed. That night, I called the customer to ask if he was satisfied with the work or needed any help operating the garage door opener. Two weeks later I called again — just to check if things were still fine."

DO YOU REMEMBER?

In "How to Create Problems and Drive Customers Away," we listed eight statements to avoid — and also asked you to add your own to that list. How many of them can you recall? Write them down.

1. _____

2. _____

3. _____

4. _____

5. _____

6. _____

7. _____

8. _____

Here are the "Three Quick Tips for Preventing Problems" discussed on page 79. See if you can recall how each technique can be implemented.

1. Avoid the caller Ping-Pong effect.

_____

_____

_____

2. Stop problems at the point of sale.

_____

_____

_____

3. Repair costs? Explain to gain.

_____

_____

_____

Based on what you've learned in Session 5, again rate yourself on the following statements. When you are finished, compare your total score to the one you earned at the beginning of this session.

WEAK	**AVERAGE**	**STRONG**
1–4 points	5–7 points	8–10 points

Avoid making statements that create customer problems. _____

Abilty to overcome customer skepticism. _____

Represent product or service accurately. _____

Know steps to prevent problems before they occur. _____

Keep in touch with clients during a problem situation. _____

Treat customers as individuals. _____

Able to win back customers who have had a bad experience
with your company or its product or service. _____

Know how to prevent customers from complaining of high costs. _____

Able to spot potential problems before they occur. _____

Prevent a product or service problem from escalating. _____

Take responsibility for customer problems. _____

Able to think of a customer as a partner. _____

TOTAL RATING _____

WEAK	**FAIR**	**GOOD**	**STRONG**
Under 48	49–65	66–84	85–120

ACTION PLAN

Many of the skills are interrelated, and building from your strengths is a good place to start improving your overall abilities. But you can't afford to overlook your weaknesses either. List below your three best scores (your **strengths**) and your three lowest scores (your **weaknesses**) from the ratings on the previous page.

STRENGTHS

1. _____

2. _____

3. _____

WEAKNESSES

1. _____

2. _____

3. _____

Comparing the two lists, can you see any ways in which you can use your strengths to improve your weaknesses? If so, write them down briefly.

_____

_____

_____

Now re-examine your three biggest weaknesses. Since it's best to work on them one at a time, list them in this order: Start with the one you think will be the easiest to improve upon, followed by a more difficult one, and then the most difficult one.

Next to each, set a timetable for concentrating on them (one week, two weeks, etc.).

TIMETABLE FOR WORKING ON WEAKNESSES/IMPROVEMENT

1. _____

2. _____

3. _____

Using the ideas and information from this session, list at least one technique you can practice to improve each weakness. Also add any ideas of your own.

1. _____

2. _____

3. _____

_____

_____

If you cannot determine a technique or course of action you think will be effective, talk to your supervisor for ideas that can be applied to your specific situation.

At the end of the time frame you set for improvement on *all* of your weaknesses, look again at the skill level rating on page 86. Rate yourself once more on *all* of the statements listed. You will probably find improvement not only in your weak areas but in the others as well.

S U M M A R Y

While the proper place for problem prevention is at the beginning of the interaction with a customer or client, we've saved this session for last. Why? Because it is probably the most overlooked area in customer service training, and we wanted to leave you with these ideas fresh in your mind.

Although it's obvious, it bears repeating: The problem you prevent is the one you don't have to solve. Or to put it another way, the customer who doesn't get angry is one less tough customer for you to handle. But you do have to take action to keep that anger from occurring.

When you keep in touch with a customer during a problem situation, when you make a habit of accurately representing your product or service, or when you use any of the other skills covered in this session, you are minimizing the number of customer service problems you might otherwise have to deal with. Taking the time and effort to prevent customer problems from happening is a great way to make your job, and your life, that much easier.